AROUND THE WORLD COOKBOOK

CHARTWELL
BOOKS, INC.

Published by Chartwell Books, Inc
A Division of Book Sales, Inc.
110 Enterprise Avenue
Secaucus, New Jersey 07094

© Marshall Cavendish Limited 1985
All rights reserved.
ISBN 0–89009–891–3

INTRODUCTION

The different cuisines of the world offer new and exciting dishes, yet many cooks are deterred from trying them because of the unfamiliar ingredients and techniques involved. All the dishes in this collection have an authentic feel, yet they are made with readily available ingredients that can be bought at large supermarkets, health food stores or ethnic food stores.

With this book as a guide, you can explore a wide variety of culinary styles and learn about the traditions and customs associated with each national dish. The result will be meals that delight your family and friends, and make you a successful international cook. Try stir-fried Chinese vegetables, accompanied by spicy sauces, Australian barbecue food, nourishing soups and stews, or festive cakes and cookies from Austria and Germany. Plan a complete Indian main course with a colorful Madras curry or a delicate chicken korma, garnished with hot pickle and served with rice and poppadoms. Whatever the occasion — a dinner party, informal supper or light summer lunch — there is an unusual dish here to make it extra special.

SYMBOLS

 FREEZING When to freeze a dish

 WATCHPOINT Pitfalls to avoid during preparation

 TIME 1-2 hours

 TIME Over 2 hours

 TIME TRAP Allow extra time

CONTENTS

FRANCE

Not surprisingly, *Coq au vin* (chicken in wine) originated in Burgundy, one of the great wine-growing districts of France. The chicken is cooked with pearl onions and mushrooms in a sauce containing brandy as well as red wine. *Coq au vin* is one of the glories of French provincial cooking and features widely on menus throughout France – from the smartest restaurant to the most unpretentious bistro.

Coq au vin

SERVES 4

1 (3-3½ lb) broiler-fryer, cut up into 8 pieces (see Cook's tip)
2 tablespoons all-purpose flour
salt and freshly ground black pepper
6 tablespoons butter
½ lb bacon slices, diced
8 pearl onions
2 cloves garlic, minced
2 cups button mushrooms
2 tablespoons brandy
1 pint robust red wine
1 cup strong chicken stock
bouquet garni

BEURRE MANIE (kneaded butter)
1 tablespoon all-purpose flour
1 tablespoon butter

1 Put the flour in a large plastic bag and season with 1 teaspoon salt and ¼ teaspoon pepper. Add the chicken pieces and shake to coat the chicken thoroughly.
2 Melt 4 tablespoons of the butter in a large Dutch oven or saucepan, add the diced bacon and sauté over moderate heat, stirring occasionally, for about 5 minutes until golden brown. Remove the bacon from the pot with a slotted spoon and reserve.
3 Add the onions and garlic to the fat in the pot and sauté gently, stirring occasionally, for about 5 minutes, until golden brown. Add mushrooms and sauté, stirring, for 1 minute. Remove vegetables from the pot with a slotted spoon and reserve with the bacon.
4 Melt the remaining butter in the pot, add the floured chicken pieces and cook over moderate heat, turning, for 3-4 minutes until brown on all sides. Remove the chicken pieces from the heat.
5 Warm the brandy in a small saucepan and pour over the chicken. Ignite immediately with a match, shaking the pot once or twice until the flames die down.
6 Return the reserved vegetables and bacon to the casserole, pour in the wine and stock and add the bouquet garni. Bring to a boil, stirring, then cover, lower the heat and simmer gently for 30-40 minutes, or until the chicken is tender and cooked through (the juices run clear when the flesh is pierced in the thickest part with a fine skewer).
7 Meanwhile, preheat the oven to 225°F. Make the beurre manié: Blend the flour and butter together with a spatula to make a smooth paste, then cut the paste into pea-size pieces.
8 When the chicken pieces are cooked, transfer them with a slotted spoon to a platter and keep warm in the oven. Remove the onions and mushrooms in the same way and keep warm with the chicken. Discard the bouquet garni.
9 Beat the pieces of beurre manié into the sauce in the pot. Simmer over low heat, beating constantly, until the sauce thickens.
10 Simmer for 1-2 minutes, then return the chicken, onions and mushrooms to the pot and turn to coat in the sauce. Serve at once, straight from the pot (see Serving ideas).

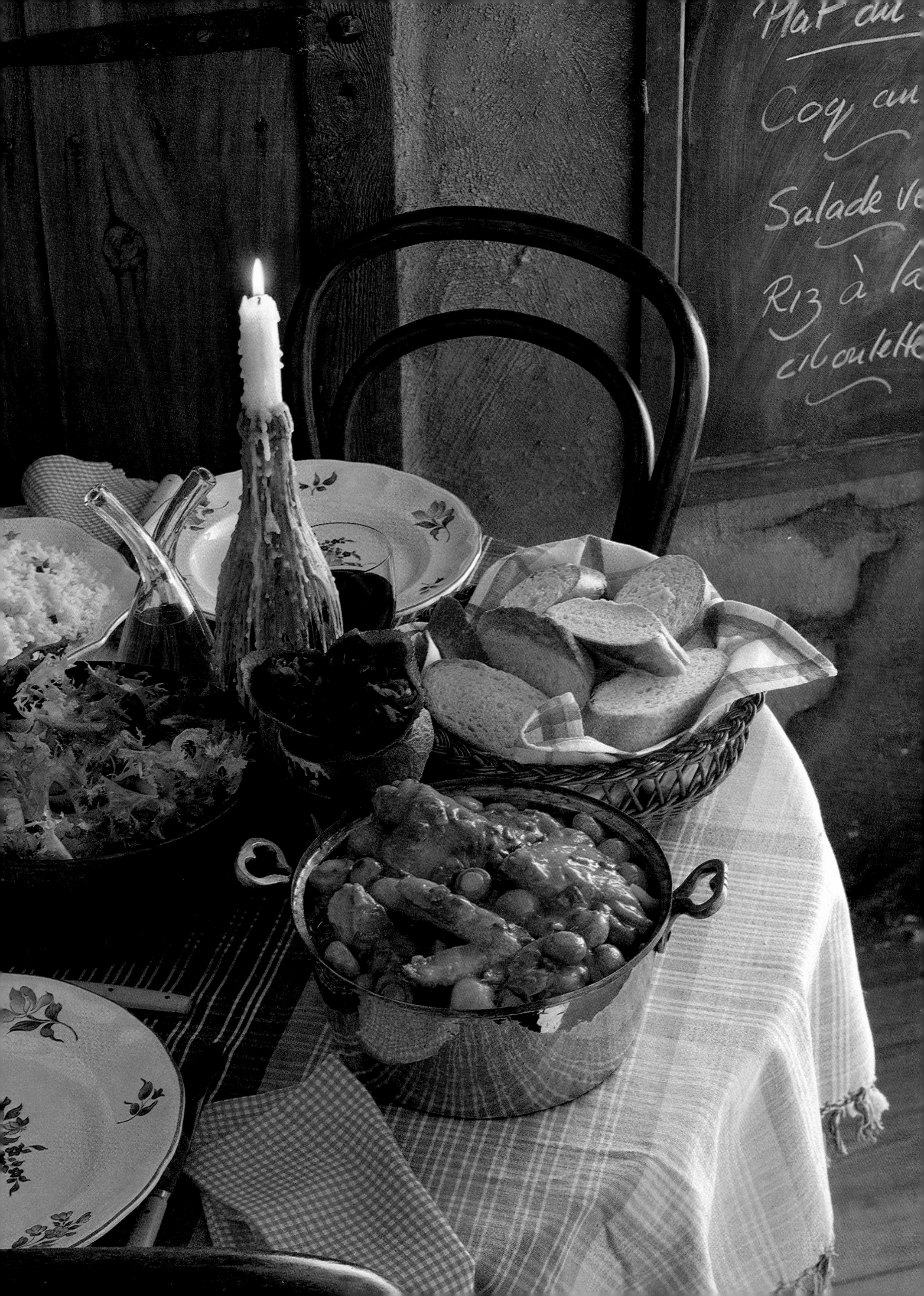
Plat du
Coq au
Salade ve
Riz à la
ciboulette

Sole Véronique is a classic French dish of lightly poached fillets of sole served in a creamy white wine sauce, garnished with tiny green grapes. The color of the dish is subtly pale and the flavor is delicate, the grapes giving a juicy texture that complements the softness of the fish. It makes a perfect main course for a summer dinner party.

The name Véronique was originally given to this dish by Monsieur Malley, head chef at the Ritz hotel in London at the turn of the century. Monsieur Malley decided to add grapes to the white wine sauce in a fish dish he was preparing for a party at the hotel. The dish was named after the baby girl born to his assistant chef on the day of the party, and since then the term (Véronique) has been used to describe any savory dish cooked with white wine and grapes.

Sole Véronique

SERVES 4

3 (¾ lb) sole, skinned and each cut in 4 fillets, bones and trimmings reserved (see Buying guide)
10 black peppercorns
1 onion, sliced
1 celery stalk, sliced
1 bay leaf
⅔ cup dry white wine
¼ lb seedless green grapes (see Buying guide)
2 tablespoons butter
¼ cup all-purpose flour
1¼ cups milk
¼ cup heavy cream
salt and freshly ground white pepper

1 Make the stock: Place the fish bones and trimmings in a large kettle. Add the peppercorns, onion, celery, bay leaf and white wine, and pour in just enough fresh cold water to cover the bones. Bring to a boil, reduce the heat and simmer for about 20 minutes. ☐

2 Strain the fish stock into a clean kettle and boil to reduce by half.

3 Preheat the oven to 350°F.

4 Trim any untidy edges from the fish fillets, then place them in a single layer, skinned side downward, in an ovenproof dish. Tuck both ends of each fillet under, so that the fillets are all the same length.

5 Pour over enough of the reduced fish stock just to cover the fish. Cover the dish with a lid or foil and cook in the oven for 15 minutes.

6 Meanwhile, plunge the grapes into boiling water for 5 seconds, drain and remove skins.

7 When the fish is cooked, turn the oven down to 275°F. Carefully remove the poached fillets from the baking dish, place them on an ovenproof plate with the grapes and keep warm in the oven. ☐ Strain the cooking liquid into a clean saucepan and boil vigorously to reduce by half.

Measure out ⅔ cup in a liquid measure.

8 To make the sauce: Melt the butter in a saucepan, sprinkle in the flour and stir over low heat for 1-2 minutes until straw-colored. Remove from the heat and gradually stir in the milk and the ⅔ cup reduced cooking liquid. Return to the heat and bring to a boil, stirring constantly. Reduce the heat and simmer for 2 minutes, until thick and smooth. Remove from the heat and stir in the cream and half the grapes with salt and pepper to taste.

9 Arrange the fillets of sole on a warmed flat serving dish. Pour the sauce evenly over the fish and scatter the remaining grapes on top to make an attractive garnish.

TIME
Preparation, including making the stock and sauce, takes about 1 hour. Cooking the fish in the oven takes 15 minutes.

 BUYING GUIDE
Imported Dover sole has a particularly fine texture, but is very expensive. Flounder (lemon or gray sole) is cheaper, and can be used as a substitute, if wished. If your supplier fillets the fish for you, remember to ask him to give you the bones and trimmings for stock.

The best grapes to use are either White Malaga (available September-November) or else Thompson Seedless (available June-January). Both these Californian grapes are seedless. If neither is available, use ordinary green or white grapes; cut them in half, if liked, and then remove the seeds after peeling.

 VARIATION
Fresh sole is preferable, but you can also use frozen fillets. In this case, do not make the fish stock as described in stage 1; just place the thawed fillets in an ovenproof dish, add the peppercorns, sliced onion and celery, bay leaf and ⅔ cup white wine and fresh cold water just to cover. Cover the dish and cook in the oven for 15 minutes. Continue from stage 6 and in stage 7 measure out ⅔ cup cooking liquid to make the sauce. The result will be good, but the sauce will not be quite so thick and flavorsome; a perfect sauce needs to be made with a twice-reduced fish stock.

COOK'S TIP
To remove the fishy smell from the kettles or saucepans used for the stock, soak the saucepans overnight in water with a little dry mustard dissolved in it.

WATCHPOINTS
When making fish stock, never simmer the bones for longer than 25 minutes, or the stock tends to become bitter.

It is important to warm the grapes through thoroughly in the oven. However, fish tends to overcook easily, and should not be kept warm for too long. Try not to leave it in the oven for more than 10 minutes. Have everything ready to make the sauce, to ensure that there are no unnecessary delays.

SERVING IDEAS
Serve a crisp green vegetable to complement the softness of the fish fillets. Lightly cooked broccoli or zucchini would be ideal. Plainly boiled or steamed tiny new potatoes are also a delicious accompaniment.

•325 calories per portion

The true king of casseroles, Boeuf à la bourguignonne gets both its name and its wonderful mellow richness from the full-bodied red Burgundy wine in which it is first marinated and then slowly simmered. Much of the world's most famous food and wine comes from this region, which stretches southeast of Paris up to the Swiss border.

The secret of making a Boeuf à la bourguignonne, that would do a Burgundian chef credit, lies not in elaborate cooking methods but in carefully chosen ingredients, plenty of time for marinating and long, gentle cooking. So choose good-quality meat, a true Burgundy wine such as Côte de Beaune, Savigny or Pommard, and do not try to rush the simmering process.

To serve Boeuf à la bourguignonne in true French style, accompany it simply with plenty of fresh crusty bread and tossed green salad. Drink a red Burgundy wine to make it a French meal to remember. Conclude the meal with a simple sherbet or creamy Camembert.

Boeuf à la bourguignonne

SERVES 4

2 lb chuck steak, cut in large pieces 4 inches long
2-3 tablespoons olive oil
6 oz diced blanched salt pork
2 medium onions, sliced
2 medium carrots, sliced
2 tablespoons all-purpose flour
salt and freshly ground black pepper
3 tablespoons brandy (optional)
1 large clove garlic, minced
bouquet garni (parsley, thyme, bay leaf)
about ⅔ cup boiling water

MARINADE
1¼ cups red Burgundy wine
2 tablespoons olive oil
½ teaspoon dried mixed herbs

TO FINISH
2 tablespoons butter
½ lb whole pearl onions
2 cups button mushrooms
6 tablespoons red wine
1 teaspoon brown sugar

1 Place the chuck steak in a shallow dish. Add the marinade ingredients and turn the meat in them several times. Cover and let stand in a cool place for at least 3 hours, turning the meat occasionally.

2 Preheat the oven to 350°F.

3 Heat 2 tablespoons olive oil in a large skillet over moderate heat, add the salt pork and sauté until golden brown. Remove with slotted spoon, drain on absorbent kitchen paper.

4 Turn the heat down to low, add the sliced onions and carrots and sauté for about 15 minutes until the onions are golden. Remove with a slotted spoon and drain on the paper with the bacon.

5 Remove the meat from the marinade and drain thoroughly in a strainer, making sure you save all the liquid. Pat the meat dry with absorbent kitchen paper.

6 Add another tablespoon olive oil to the skillet if needed. Increase the heat and sauté the meat briskly until brown on all sides.

7 Season the flour with salt and pepper, then sprinkle over the meat. Cook the meat for another 5 minutes, turning it constantly. Stir in the reserved marinade and the brandy (if using) and bring to a boil, scraping up all the sediment from the side and bottom of the pan.

8 Transfer the meat and marinade to a Dutch oven. Add the reserved bacon, onions and carrots with the garlic and bouquet garni, then pour in enough boiling water just to cover the meat and vegetables. Bring to a boil, then cover the pot and transfer it to the oven. Cook for 2 hours or until the meat is tender but still firm. Check the contents of the pot occasionally and add a little more boiling water if too dry.

9 To finish: Melt the butter in a skillet over moderate heat. Add the whole pearl onions and mushrooms and sauté for 2-3 minutes. Pour in the wine, stir in the sugar and bring to a boil. Stir this mixture into the pot, replace the lid and continue cooking for a further 30 minutes until the meat and onions are tender.

10 Skim off any excess fat from the pot with a skimmer or slotted spoon. Discard the bouquet garni, then taste and adjust seasoning. Serve the dish hot, straight from the Dutch oven.

Profiteroles – little choux paste puffs – make an impressive-looking dessert. The paste swells into crisp, hollow shells which, in France, are traditionally filled with sweetened whipped cream. Other more unusual fillings can be used, such as the ice cream in this recipe. For maximum impact, pile the profiteroles high and pour chocolate sauce over them.

Profiteroles

MAKES 22

1 cup plus 2 tablespoons bread flour
  (see Watchpoints)
2 teaspoons superfine sugar
1 cup water
½ cup butter, cut in small pieces
4 eggs
1 teaspoon brandy or rum
  (optional)
1 quart vanilla ice cream
  (see Cook's tip)
beaten egg and sugar, for glaze

CHOCOLATE SAUCE

9 squares (9 oz) semisweet chocolate
¾ cup milk
piece of vanilla bean
2 tablespoons heavy cream
3 tablespoons butter
½ cup sugar

1 Preheat the oven to 400°F.

2 Sift the flour and sugar twice, then sift onto a sheet of waxed paper. Set aside.

3 Put water into a deep saucepan and add the butter. Place the pan over low heat and warm gently until all the butter has melted, then increase the heat to bring the liquid to a rolling boil. Draw the pan aside immediately and shoot in the flour mixture all at once. Lower the heat and return the pan to the range immediately then, using a large wooden spoon, beat the paste vigorously until the flour has cooked and the mixture is smooth. It must not look grainy and should roll cleanly off the side of the pan into a ball, leaving a floury film over the base. [!] Remove from the heat and let cool in the saucepan for about 5 minutes.

4 Break 1 egg into a cup and beat lightly with a fork, then pour onto the flour paste and beat thoroughly to blend. Continue in the same way with the remaining eggs, adding only a little at a time toward the end, so the mixture does not get too moist (you may even need a little more egg if conditions are very dry. [!] The finished paste should be quite firm but elastic – it will drop from a spoon slowly when jerked. Beat the paste well until it is shiny and smooth. Beat in brandy or rum if using.

5 Chill a flat baking sheet: Hold it under cold running water for a few moments, shake off excess moisture but leave damp. Place teaspoonfuls of the paste, about 1 inch in size, at 2 inch intervals on the wet sheet; leaving these large spaces to allow the profiteroles room to expand. Lightly brush a little beaten egg on each one and sprinkle over a pinch of sugar.

6 Place sheet in the oven [!] and bake for about 20 minutes until the profiteroles are well browned all over and feel very light and hollow when picked up.[!]

7 Remove the sheet from the oven. Pierce each puff with a skewer or knife to release the steam inside. Let cool on a wire rack.

8 Meanwhile, make chocolate sauce: Break the chocolate in pieces and place in a heatproof bowl over a pan one quarter full of gently simmering water (the water must not touch the bowl). Heat gently until the chocolate has melted.

9 Pour the milk into a separate saucepan and add the vanilla bean. Bring to the boiling point, then add the cream and bring back to a boil. Off heat, remove the vanilla bean, then stir in the melted chocolate, butter and sugar. Return to the heat and boil for a few seconds, stirring until thickened.

10 Cut each profiterole in half. Cut the ice cream into 22 small cubes and put 1 cube into each profiterole (see Cook's tip). Pile profiteroles attractively onto a glass or china serving platter. Pour over the hot chocolate sauce and serve at once.

Cook's Notes

TIME
Preparing and baking the choux paste takes 40 minutes; allow 30 minutes for cooling, during which time the chocolate sauce can be made. Allow 5 minutes for assembly.

WATCHPOINTS
Use bread flour if possible, as it has a higher gluten content than all-purpose flour, giving more volume and crispness.

The paste mixture only takes a few seconds to cook. If allowed to cook too long the finished profiteroles will be heavy.

If the choux mixture is too moist it will fail to rise properly.

Choux paste puffs can burn very easily so it is important that the oven temperature is correct. If your oven is inclined to overheat, use a layer of foil or a second baking sheet underneath for added protection.

Do not open the oven door until the puffs have cooked for at least 15 minutes. If not cooked sufficiently, the delicate puffs may collapse.

COOK'S TIP
The ice cream must be as hard as possible – if possible, avoid soft-serve ice cream. If you have to use soft serve, spoon it into the hollowed choux puffs and serve as quickly as possible.

●205 calories per profiterole

MAKING CHOUX PASTE

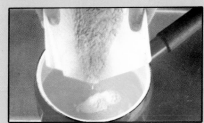

1 *Bring the water and butter to a boil. Remove from heat and shoot in the sifted flour and sugar.*

2 *Scoop mixture onto a teaspoon. Using back of another spoon, push mixture onto baking sheet.*

There are many delicious versions of *Tarte aux pommes,* the celebrated French apple flan. One has a creamed almond mixture the French call *frangipane* underneath the apples; another has a puréed apple base on which the apple slices are arranged. In this popular version, a cream and egg custard is poured over the apples in the rich pie shell.

Tarte aux pommes

SERVES 6

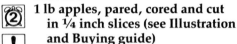
1 lb apples, pared, cored and cut in ¼ inch slices (see Illustration and Buying guide)
¼ cup sweet butter
3 eggs
2 tablespoons superfine sugar
pinch of ground cinnamon
pinch of freshly grated nutmeg
1¼ cups light cream

DOUGH
1½ cups all-purpose flour
pinch of salt
6 tablespoons superfine sugar
¼ cup sweet butter, softened
3 large egg yolks

GLAZE
3 tablespoons apricot jam
2 tablespoons Kirsch, Calvados or brandy

1 Make the dough: Sift the flour and salt into a bowl. Make a well in the center and add the sugar, butter and egg yolks.
2 Using the fingertips of one hand, or a fork, gradually work the butter, sugar and egg yolks together. Gradually incorporate the flour until the dough forms a ball. Wrap it in plastic wrap and refrigerate for 30 minutes (see Cook's tips).
3 Meanwhile, make the glaze: Put the jam in a small saucepan with the Kirsch. Stir over gentle heat until the jam has dissolved. Press the mixture through a nylon strainer and set aside.
4 Preheat the oven to 425°F.
5 Roll out the dough on a lightly floured surface to a round 1 inch larger than a loose-bottomed 10 inch fluted pie pan. Roll the dough round

loosely around the rolling pin, then carefully unroll it over the pie pan. Press the dough into the pan, molding it well into the fluted edge. Trim any excess dough. Chill the lined pie pan in the refrigerator for 15-20 minutes.
6 Place a large circle of waxed paper or foil in the pie shell and weight it down with baking beans. Bake blind in the oven for 15 minutes, then remove from the oven and lower the oven heat to 400°F.
7 While the pie shell is baking, prepare the filling: Melt the butter in a large skillet; add the apple slices and cook gently for 4-5 minutes until they just begin to soften, turning them carefully with a fish turner.

8 Arrange the apple slices (see Illustration and Cook's tips) in the partially-baked pie shell. Beat together the eggs, sugar, spices and cream and pour evenly over the slices. Do this carefully to avoid spoiling the design.
9 Bake the flan in the oven for 25-30 minutes until the custard is just set and firm to the touch.
10 Meanwhile, reheat the apricot glaze in a small saucepan. Bring just to the boiling point.
11 Let the apple flan cool slightly, then brush the surface with the hot glaze. Let cool slightly, remove from pan and place on serving platter. Serve Tarte aux pommes warm or cold.

Cook's Notes

 TIME
Preparing and chilling the pie shell takes about 50 minutes (make the glaze during chilling). Baking blind and preparing the filling take about 15 minutes; filling the pie shell and glazing about 30 minutes, and baking in the oven about 30 minutes.

WATCHPOINTS
If the dough breaks, simply press the edges back together again.
Be careful not to overcook the apple slices or they will lose their shape and become mushy when baked.

BUYING GUIDE
The best variety of apple for this flan is Rome Beauty, which holds its shape well. Alternatively, use Newtown Pippins, Jonathans or Winesaps.

 COOK'S TIPS
Work the dough as little as possible to prevent it from becoming sticky. It will be quite soft, and chilling helps it firm up.
The classic French way to arrange the apple slices is in a spiral, starting at the center of the flan. But the flan also looks very attractive if the apples are arranged in circles, starting at the edge of the pan.

 FREEZING
Flash freeze the flan until solid. Remove from pie pan, cover with plastic wrap, overwrap in foil, seal, label and freeze for up to 3 months. To serve: Unwrap, replace in pie pan, and cover with foil. Bake in the oven at 400°F for 20 minutes. Serve the flan warm or cold.

●455 calories per portion

PREPARING AND ARRANGING APPLES

Cut apples in half, cut out core with a small sharp knife.

Pare the apples, then cut lengthwise in thick slices.

Starting at center of flan, arrange slices overlapping in a spiral shape.

ENGLAND

Regal enough for any occasion, crown roast of lamb was a popular Edwardian dinner-party dish and is still one of the easiest and most decorative ways of serving a set number of people.

Allow each person 2 ribs when buying the roast and you know in advance how many guests to ask!

The traditional apricot stuffing has an unusual spicy yet mild flavoring of coriander – a spice once grown in southern England and much loved in the 18th century.

Crown roast of lamb

SERVES 6-8
2 lamb rib roasts with 6-8 ribs each, with backbone removed (see Cook's tip)
¼ cup butter, melted
salt and freshly ground black pepper

STUFFING
1 tablespoon butter
1 tablespoon vegetable oil
1 small onion, minced
4 cups soft white bread crumbs
1 tablespoon coriander seeds (see Buying guide)
⅔ cup dried apricots, soaked overnight, then drained and roughly chopped
⅓ cup seedless raisins
½ cup chopped walnuts
1 tablespoon chopped parsley
beaten egg, to bind

GRAVY
⅔ cup chicken stock
⅔ cup dry white wine or hard cider
2 tablespoons currant jelly

1 To make the stuffing: Heat the butter and oil in a small saucepan. Add the onion and sauté gently until soft but not brown.
2 Stir in the bread crumbs, transfer to a bowl and let cool.
3 Crush the coriander seeds in a grinder or pestle and mortar, then add to the bread crumbs with the remaining stuffing ingredients and salt and pepper to taste. Stir well to mix, then bind with beaten egg.
4 Preheat the oven to 400°F.

5 To prepare the meat: See Preparation, or ask your butcher to make up the crown roast beforehand.
6 Stand the crown roast in a roasting pan. Season the melted butter with salt

and freshly ground black pepper and brush about half on the outside of the roast. Pour the rest into the roasting pan.

7 Fill the center of the roast with the stuffing and cover the top and each protruding bone end with foil.

8 Roast the meat in the oven for about 10 minutes, then lower the heat to 350°F and continue to cook for 1½-2 hours, depending on how well cooked you like your lamb.

9 Transfer the roast to a warmed serving dish and keep hot. Drain off the excess fat from the roasting pan, then transfer to the top of the range to make the gravy. Add the stock and wine to the pan and bring to a boil, stirring to scrape off any brown pieces from the base of the pan. Allow to bubble and reduce slightly, then add the currant jelly and stir until it melts. Taste and adjust seasoning, then pour into a sauceboat and keep hot.

10 Remove the foil from the bone ends of the meat, then decorate each bone with a frill, a small cherry tomato or a pearl onion parboiled and lightly browned in butter. To serve, carve the roast into ribs, allowing 2 per person.

Cook's Notes

 TIME
30 minutes to prepare the stuffing; the apricots need to be soaked overnight. The meat takes 30 minutes to prepare, and cooking time is 1¾-2¼ hours.

 COOK'S TIP
Most good butchers will prepare a crown roast for you if given at least 48 hours notice. Some will even make a stuffing for you as well.

 BUYING GUIDE
If coriander seeds are not available, commercially ground coriander is a slightly milder substitute.

●510 calories per portion

TO PREPARE A CROWN ROAST

1 *Remove the fell on the fatty side of the roasts.*

3 *On meaty side, make slits between rib bases.*

2 *Remove fat and meat from bone ends. Cut away gristle and meat in between. Scrape clean.*

4 *Sew roasts together. Fat inside, bend roast around to form a ring. Sew together.*

IRELAND

In the best traditions of regional cooking, Irish stew was originally made from ingredients raised or grown locally on the farms. The toughest cuts of mutton or goat became tender during long, slow cooking and imparted their rich, strong flavour to potatoes and onions, the only vegetables included in an authentic Irish stew. Nowadays the stew is made with lamb, and other vegetables such as carrots, turnips or celery may be included.

Irish stew

SERVES 4-6

**3-3½ lb rib or shoulder lamb
  chops, trimmed of excess fat
  (see Buying guide)**
**2 lb potatoes, cut in ¼ inch
  slices**
1 lb onions, sliced
1 tablespoon chopped fresh parsley
**1 tablespoon chopped fresh thyme,
  or 1 teaspoon dried thyme**
salt and freshly ground black pepper
2 cups water
**1 tablespoon chopped fresh parsley,
  for garnish**

1 Preheat the oven to 275°F.
2 Arrange one-third of the sliced potatoes in a layer in the base of a large casserole. Add a layer of one-third of the sliced onions, sprinkle with some of the parsley and thyme and season with salt and pepper. Arrange half the lamb chops on top and season with more salt and pepper. Make a further layer each of potatoes and onions. Sprinkle with herbs and season with salt and pepper. Arrange the remaining lamb chops on top and season with more salt and pepper. Cover the meat with the remaining onions and herbs and arrange a final layer of potatoes on top, overlapping the slices so that they cover the onions completely (see Illustration).
3 Pour over the water and cover the casserole tightly with a piece of foil and then with the lid.
4 Cook the casserole in the oven for 3 hours, checking from time to time to make sure that the liquid has not evaporated too much. If the casserole does begin to look dry, add a little boiling water to moisten it slightly.
5 Remove the casserole from the oven and remove the foil. Run a knife around the edge of the casserole, garnish with chopped parsley and serve at once.

LAYERING POTATOES

Arrange the sliced potatoes over-lapping to form a "crust" on top of the final layer of sliced onions.

Cook's Notes

 TIME
Preparation takes about 30 minutes, cooking in the oven 3 hours.

 BUYING GUIDE
Rib or shoulder chops give a very tasty sauce, much of the flavor coming from the bones which are cooked as part of the dish. Neck of lamb, a less expensive cut of lamb, also gives good results. Ask the butcher to chop it into serving-size pieces.

 SERVING IDEAS
A simple dish of root vegetables such as sliced carrots or tiny white turnips is ideal to serve with Irish stew. Serve also boiled shredded cabbage tossed in butter and chunks of warm homemade Irish soda bread.
  A glass of beer goes well with Irish stew.

COOK'S TIP
If you do not wish to use the oven, this is an ideal dish to cook in an electric Dutch oven. Follow manufacturer's directions for timing.
  The stew may also be cooked on top of the range in a large heavy-bottomed saucepan. Grease the pan before layering the ingredients in it, then cook for 2½-3 hours over very low heat. If possible, stand the pan on a flame tamer.

●925 calories per portion

SCOTLAND

Although shortbread is very popular all the year around and in all parts of Great Britain, it is particularly associated with Scotland. It is served at Christmas time and at Hogmanay when it is offered to the first callers of the New Year in return for the good luck they are thought to bring.

Shortbread is quick and easy to make, but relies for its success on long, slow baking and top-quality ingredients – butter is essential to make each piece literally melt in the mouth.

Traditionally, shortbread is shaped in attractive wooden molds, the most usual being decorated with a thistle design, but it can also be shaped by hand.

Shortbread

MAKES 2 SHORTBREADS

2 cups all-purpose flour
good pinch of salt
⅔ cup rice flour
1 cup butter
½ cup superfine sugar
superfine sugar, for finishing

1 Preheat the oven to 180°C. Line 2 baking sheets with ungreased waxed paper.
2 Sift together the flour, salt and rice flour onto a plate.
3 Using your fingertips, rub the butter and sugar together on a pastry board or marble slab until well blended. [!]
4 Gradually work the flour mixture into the butter and sugar, keeping the mixing as light as possible, until all the ingredients are blended together into a large, smooth ball of dough.
5 Divide dough in half and place on prepared baking sheets. Or place each piece of dough in a 7 inch shortbread mold (see Preparation). Pat each piece out with the heel of the hand to form a 6½ inch round ½-¾ inch thick (see Illustration).
6 Neaten the edge if slightly cracked by pressing together with a knife, then crimp the edge in the traditional way, using a finger and thumb (see Illustration).

SHAPING AND FINISHING SHORTBREAD

1 Use the heel of the hand to shape the shortbread carefully into a round.

2 Use finger and thumb to crimp the edge of the shortbread decoratively.

7 Prick the shortbread all over in circles with a fork so that it does not rise during cooking. Place a 7 inch flan ring around each shortbread, if liked, to keep edge neat during baking.
8 Bake in the center of the oven for 40-45 minutes or until pale golden brown, covering if necessary with waxed paper toward the end of baking to avoid overbrowning the shortbread (see Cook's tip).
9 Remove the shortbreads from the oven and immediately score each in 8 sections with a sharp knife, taking care not to cut right through. Sprinkle the top of each shortbread with sugar. Let cool slightly, then transfer to a wire rack until quite cold. To serve, cut right through the scored sections or break them with your fingers.

WALES

Bara brith (pronounced "breeth") means "speckled bread" in Welsh, and is a spiced fruit loaf traditional to all Celtic countries. In Wales, country people have always been famed for their sweet breads, and Bara brith was a customary treat at Christmas, Easter and harvest time. Originally it was made with yeast, but self-rising flour is quicker and easier to use.

Bara brith

MAKES 2 LOAVES
(see Economy)
 1⅓ cups golden raisins
(see Cook's tips)
 ⅔ cup dried currants
⅔ cup seedless raisins
2½ cups light brown sugar
2½ cups warm strong tea, strained
1 egg, lightly beaten
6 cups self-rising flour (see Cook's tips)
2 teaspoons ground apple pie spice
vegetable oil, for greasing
1 tablespoon honey, to glaze

1 Put the golden raisins, dried currants, raisins and sugar in a bowl. Pour in the tea and stir well. Cover with a clean dish towel and let stand overnight.
2 Preheat the oven to 325°F.
3 Grease and line with waxed paper two 9 × 5 inch loaf pans (see Illustration). Grease the lining paper.
4 Stir the beaten egg well into the fruit and brown sugar mixture. Sift together the flour and spice, then stir lightly into the batter until thoroughly combined.
5 Divide the batter equally between the prepared pans. Smooth the surface of each.
6 Bake the loaves in the oven for 1½ hours, then lower the heat to 275°F and bake for a further 1½ hours, until a warmed fine skewer inserted into the loaves comes out clean.
7 Leave the loaves for a few minutes until cool enough to handle, then invert them onto a wire rack. Turn the loaves the right way up.
8 Put the honey in a small saucepan and heat very gently. Brush the tops of the warm loaves, to glaze. Let stand until completely cold.

Cook's Notes

TIME
Allow overnight soaking time. Preparation then takes about 15 minutes. Baking takes 3 hours and glazing 5 minutes.

ECONOMY
As Bara brith stores and freezes well, it is well worth baking 2 loaves, to save on fuel. If you prefer to make just 1 loaf, you can of course simply halve the quantities given in the recipe.

COOK'S TIPS
Just 1 or 2 types of dried fruit may be used, providing the total amount is 2⅔ cups.
If you prefer, use all-purpose flour sifted with 2 tablespoons baking powder.
The bread may be eaten as soon as it is completely cold, but the flavor and texture improve if it is stored in an airtight tin for 1 week.

SERVING IDEAS
Serve cut in slices and spread with butter. Honey or jam go well with Bara brith for tea, or try it with a wedge of Caerphilly or Cheddar cheese for a snack lunch.

FREEZING
Flash freeze the baked glazed loaves until the glaze is firm, then wrap in foil, seal, label and freeze for up to 6 months. To serve: Unwrap and thaw at room temperature for 4-6 hours.

● 3030 calories per loaf

TO LINE A LOAF PAN

1 *Use base of pan to mark waxed paper with pencil. Cut out rectangle along line.*

2 *Cut waxed paper strip 2 inches wider than pan depth and long enough to go around pan.*

3 *Fold in ½ inch border along one long side of strip. Snip as far as fold.*

4 *Fit strip inside greased pan with snipped border on base. Place waxed paper rectangle on top.*

FINLAND

In Finland, the traditional food for a family feast is a casserole of mixed meats accompanied by rice-filled pasties. Both these dishes come from Karelia, a region that was once in eastern Finland but is now part of the Soviet Union. On farms, the hotpot was put into a hot brick oven early in the morning and left to simmer all day until the dish was cooked and the oven nearly cold. Tasty and warming, these dishes are ideal food for cold days.

Karelian hotpot

SERVES 6-8

- 1 lb chuck steak, cut in 1 inch cubes
- 1 lb boneless shoulder of lamb, cut in 1 inch cubes
- 1 lb boneless shoulder or loin of pork, cut in 1 inch cubes
- ¾ lb lamb kidneys, halved, cores removed
- 3 large onions, thickly sliced
- 1 teaspoon salt
- 2 teaspoons ground allspice
- 2½ cups hot beef stock

1 Preheat the oven to 400°F.
2 Put all the cubed meat and the kidneys into a Dutch oven and mix well. Top with the sliced onions.
3 Add the salt and allspice to the hot stock. Stir well to mix and pour into the pot.
4 Cover tightly and cook in the oven for about 30 minutes or until the stock is bubbling. Turn the oven down to 325°F and cook for a further 3½-4 hours until the meats are very tender. Stir well, taste and adjust seasoning (the dish should be quite salty). Serve hot with the pasties.

Karelian pasties

MAKES 12-14 PASTIES
- 1¼ cups rye flour (see Buying guide)
- 1¼ cups all-purpose flour
- ½ teaspoon salt
- ⅔ cup cold water

FILLING
- ⅔ cup water
- ¼ cup short-grain rice
- 1¼ cups milk
- ¼ teaspoon salt

GLAZE
- 2 tablespoons water
- 2 tablespoons butter

TO SERVE
- ¼ cup butter, softened
- 2 hard-cooked eggs, mashed

1 First make the filling: Bring the water to a boil over high heat. Add the rice, milk and salt and bring back to a boil, stirring. Lower the heat, cover the pan and simmer very gently, stirring occasionally, for about 45 minutes or until all the liquid is absorbed and the mixture is thick and creamy. Let cool completely.
2 To make the pastry: Sift the rye and all-purpose flours into a large bowl with the salt. Add the water, and quickly mix with one hand to form a stiff dough.
3 Knead the dough for 1-2 minutes until it leaves your hand cleanly as you work it. Add more flour or water if necessary. Wrap in plastic wrap and refrigerate the dough for 30 minutes.
4 Preheat the oven to 475°F. Dust a large baking sheet with rye flour.
5 Roll the pastry on a floured board and cut, shape and fill the pasties (see Illustration). Transfer to the prepared baking sheet.
6 Bake in the oven for 10-15 minutes until the undersides of the pasties are light-brown and the rice filling is set and light golden on top.
7 Meanwhile, make the glaze: Boil the water and add the butter. Heat until the butter has melted.
8 As soon as the pasties are cooked, dip them in the butter and water mixture and turn them until coated all over to soften the pastry.
9 To serve: Mix the soft butter with the mashed hard-cooked eggs and spoon on top of the warm pasties. Serve at once.

TO SHAPE PASTIES

1 On a board floured with rye flour, roll the pastry into a long sausage about ¾ inches in diameter. Cut in ¾ inch lengths.

2 Roll each piece into a thin oval about 6 × 4 inches.
Spread 1 tablespoon filling over the center.

3 Fold in and flute the pastry edges, leaving a little filling showing in the center.

NORWAY

Fish in many forms – fresh, smoked, salted and pickled – is a staple of the Norwegian diet. There are hundred of Norwegian fish recipes, but poached fish balls or *fiskebollar* is one of the most popular. For everyday meals they are served plain, but for special occasions they are served with a shrimp sauce, either as an hors d'oeuvre or main course accompanied by mashed potatoes and another root vegetable such as glazed rutabagas.

Fiskebollar

SERVES 4
750 g/1½ lb pollock, filleted and skinned (see Buying guide)
sea salt
freshly ground black pepper
¼ teaspoon ground mace
large pinch of freshly grated nutmeg
3 tablespoons cornstarch
¼ cup light cream
3 cups milk (see Variations)

SAUCE
2 tablespoons butter
¼ cup all-purpose flour
1 cup cooked shelled shrimp, thawed if frozen

FOR GARNISH
dill sprigs
few shrimp in shells (optional)

1 Grind the fish by passing it twice through the fine blades of a meat grinder or by working it in a food processor.
2 Transfer the ground fish to a large bowl. Add 1 teaspoon sea salt, a generous grinding of black pepper, the mace, nutmeg, cornstarch and cream. Beat with a fork for 5-10 minutes until the fish mixture is very smooth.
3 Divide the mixture into 20 portions. Roll each one between the hands to an evenly shaped ball.
4 Preheat the oven to 225°F.
5 Pour the milk into a large wide saucepan. Season with salt and pepper and bring just to a boil. Lower the heat and, using a slotted spoon, carefully put the fish balls into the pan. Simmer, uncovered, for 10-15 minutes or until the fish balls are firm and cooked through.
6 Off heat, remove the fish balls with a slotted spoon and arrange them on a warmed large serving platter. Keep them warm in the oven while making the sauce.
7 Measure 1¼ cups of the cooking liquid into a pitcher. Melt the butter in a small saucepan. Sprinkle in the flour and stir over low heat for 1-2 minutes until straw-colored. Off heat, gradually stir in the cooking liquid. Return to the heat and simmer, stirring, until thick and smooth. Add the shelled shrimp, taste and adjust seasoning, then simmer for 1-2 minutes, stirring, until the shrimp are heated through.
8 Spoon the sauce over the fish balls. Garnish with dill and unshelled shrimp, if liked, and serve at once, while piping hot.

Glazed rutabagas

SERVES 4
1 lb rutabagas, cut in 1½ inch cubes
2 tablespoons butter
2 teaspoons light corn syrup
1 teaspoon molasses
salt and freshly ground black pepper

1 Melt the butter in a Dutch oven, add the rutabagas and sauté quickly over brisk heat, turning, to brown. Add the syrup and molasses and turn to coat the rutabagas.
2 Season with salt, lower heat and cook very gently, turning occasionally, for about 30 minutes. Season with pepper and transfer to a warmed serving dish. Serve at once, with the fiskebollar.

Cook's Notes

Fiskebollar

TIME
Preparation takes about 30 minutes. Cooking time is only about 25 minutes.

BUYING GUIDE
Pollock is a member of the cod family, and is a tasty firm-fleshed fish. It is available year round on the North Atlantic seaboard.
The skin of fish fillets weighs much more than might be expected, so if buying the fish unskinned, allow an extra ¼ lb for the weight of the skin.

VARIATIONS
Fish stock may be substituted for half the quantity of milk, if liked.
The fish mixture can be shaped into 40 smaller balls and served as an appetizer for 8.

●450 calories per portion

Glazed rutabagas

TIME
Preparation takes about 5 minutes, cooking time is about 35 minutes.

BUYING GUIDE
Rutabagas, also called yellow turnips or swedes are surprisingly versatile. Try them baked in the oven, like jacket potatoes, or French-fried.
Molasses has a strong flavor and on its own would overwhelm the rutabagas. However, in combination with corn syrup it makes a delicious and unusual glaze.

●80 calories per portion

SWEDEN

Not so long ago, salmon was such common fare in Sweden that in some parts of the country contracts of employment stated that employees did not have to eat it more than three times a week! Today, however, when salmon is no longer abundant in Swedish rivers, it is considered a great delicacy, and reserved only for special occasions.

Ideally, *gravlax* (see Did you know) should be made with fresh dill which has a superb flavor. Fresh dill, however, is not readily available (despite the fact that it is very easy to grow from seed in a pot). For this reason our recipe uses the dried variety, called dillweed, which is a good substitute provided it is still aromatic.

Gravlax

SERVES 8

fresh salmon (filleted weight 1½ lb, see Buying guide)
3½ teaspoons salt
4 teaspoons sugar
1 teaspoon white peppercorns, coarsely crushed
2 tablespoons dillweed
lemon twists, for garnish

SAUCE
3 tablespoons dillweed
3 tablespoons hot water
6 tablespoons prepared mild mustard (see Buying guide)
2 tablespoons sugar
1 tablespoon red wine vinegar
2 tablespoons vegetable oil
salt and freshly ground black pepper

1 Wipe the salmon fillets with absorbent kitchen paper and remove any bones.
2 Mix the salt, sugar and peppercorns together and put about one-third in the base of a shallow dish. Lay one salmon fillet in the dish, skin side down, and sprinkle with half the remaining mixture and the dillweed. Put the second salmon fillet over the first one, skin side up. Lay its thick end on top of the thin end of the bottom fillet so that the fillets are flat (see Illustration). Rub the remaining mixture into the skin.
3 Cover the salmon with foil. Put a dish on top of the fish and put weights or heavy cans on it to press the salmon pieces together. Refrigerate for 2-3 days, turning the pieces occasionally.
4 To make the sauce: Put the dillweed in a small bowl and pour over the hot water. Leave for 5 minutes.
5 Meanwhile, mix the mustard, sugar and vinegar in a bowl, stir until the sugar has dissolved completely, then gradually add the oil and beat to a smooth sauce.
6 Drain the dillweed thoroughly, add to the sauce and season with salt and pepper to taste. Let stand in a cool place for 1 hour before serving.
7 To serve: Remove dillweed from the fish and scrape off peppercorns with a knife. Cut the fish like smoked salmon, in thin slices, or straight across into chunkier pieces (see Illustration). Discard the skin Arrange the slices on a serving platter and garnish with lemon twists. Pour the sauce into a sauceboat and pass separately.

Cook's Notes

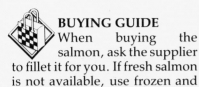

TIME
Preparation takes about 15 minutes but allow 2-3 days for marinating. Making the sauce takes about 10 minutes, but it should stand for about 1 hour before serving to let the flavors blend.

BUYING GUIDE
When buying the salmon, ask the supplier to fillet it for you. If fresh salmon is not available, use frozen and thaw it first.

Swedish mustard, which is mild and sweet, is best for this sauce, but American yellow mustard, which is also mild and more readily available, is a very good substitute.

DID YOU KNOW
It is believed that the name *gravlax* (*grav* means grave) suggests that the salmon used to be "buried" in a dark, cool cellar to marinate.

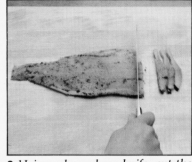

SERVING IDEAS
Serve the salmon as an appetizer with hot white toast, or thinly sliced brown bread and butter, and lemon wedges. Or serve for a light lunch with bread and a salad.

ECONOMY
Ask your supplier for the tail piece, which is sometimes cheaper.

● 240 calories per portion

MARINATING THE SALMON

Put the second fillet over the first so that the thick end of the top piece lies over the thin end of the bottom piece.

TWO METHODS OF CUTTING THE SALMON

1 *Start a few inches from the tail end and cut long, thin slices with a long, sharp knife, keeping the blade almost horizontally against the salmon.*

2 *Using a long sharp knife, cut the salmon into vertical slices about ¼ inch thick across the entire width of the salmon.*

DENMARK

Frikadeller, the egg-shaped Danish version of meatballs, are one of Denmark's most popular dishes. The Danes like to eat a light lunch of their famous open sandwiches (*smørrebrød*) and then have a hot, early evening meal. This is when Frikadeller are usually served, and most Danish families eat them at least once a week.

Frikadeller

SERVES 4

- **1 lb finely ground pork**
  (see Buying guide)
- **2 tablespoons all-purpose flour**
- **⅔ cup milk**
- **1 egg, beaten**
- **1 small onion, minced**
- **½ teaspoon ground allspice**
  (optional)
- **½ teaspoon salt**
- **½ teaspoon freshly ground black**
  pepper
- **½ cup butter, melted**
  (see Buying guide)

1 Preheat oven to 250°F.

2 Put the ground pork in a large bowl, sprinkle in the flour and very gradually stir in the milk to mix thoroughly (see Cook's tip). Stir in the egg, onion and allspice, if using, and season with salt and pepper.

3 Heat half the melted butter in a skillet. Dip a tablespoon in the remaining butter and then scoop up a heaping spoonful of the pork mixture (see Illustration).

4 Shape and sauté frikadeller over moderate heat for 5 minutes on each side, adding more butter as needed and dipping the spoon in the butter each time. Transfer to a warmed serving dish and keep hot while you sauté the remainder. Serve hot (see Serving ideas).

SHAPING FRIKADELLER

Scoop up a heaping tablespoon of ground pork mixture, then pat to a neat round against inside of bowl.

TIME
Preparation takes about 30 minutes, using ready-ground pork. Cooking takes about 40 minutes.

COOK'S TIP
The mixture should be slightly slack – not as stiff as some meatball or rissole mixtures.

VARIATIONS
Bread crumbs or crushed zwieback instead of flour and plain or carbonated water instead of milk are sometimes used to mix frikadeller.

In Denmark, frikadeller are most often made with pork, but a mixture of pork and beef or pork and veal can also be used.

Frikadeller can be made from cold leftover meat with a little ground smoked bacon added. This type is known in Denmark by the rather somber name of *døde* (dead) frikadeller.

SERVING IDEAS
In Denmark, frikadeller are usually served hot with boiled potatoes and gravy made from the pan juices. For special occasions, it is customary to serve them with sugar-browned potatoes (small potatoes browned in a caramel mixture of butter and sugar) as well as plain boiled potatoes and a second vegetable such as creamed spinach or curly kale.

Frikadeller can also be served warm with potato salad and a green salad. In Denmark, they are used cold in open sandwiches and these are a great favorite with school children in their lunch boxes.

BUYING GUIDE
Some supermarkets sell ground pork, but if it is not available, buy shoulder butt, picnic or lean trimmings from the side. Some local laws prohibit butchers from grinding pork because of the danger of trichinosis – if you grind it yourself, be sure to wash all the parts of your grinder thoroughly after use. You may need to grind the pork several times to achieve the ideal mixture for this dish.

• 580 calories per portion

BELGIUM

Waterzootje, Flemish for fisherman's soup, was originally a staple dish in the small fishing communities along the Belgian coast. Over the centuries it has become more of a chunky fish stew than a soup, and there is also a version using chicken. Cooked with white wine and cream, *Waterzootje* may be made from any kind of sea or freshwater fish.

Waterzootje

SERVES 8
4-4½ lb white fish, cleaned, filleted and skinned, trimmings reserved (see Buying guide)
3 onions, sliced
3 cloves garlic (optional)
2 cups medium white wine
juice of 1 lemon
sprig of thyme
2 sage leaves, or pinch of dried sage
2 bay leaves
6 parsley sprigs
salt and freshly ground black pepper
¼ cup butter
1 lb leeks, chopped
1 small bunch celery, chopped
4 tablespoons chopped fresh parsley

TO SERVE
2 egg yolks, beaten
¼ cup light cream
2 tablespoons chopped chives
4 extra tablespoons heavy cream (optional)

1 Put the fish heads, tails, bones and trimmings in a very large kettle with the onions, garlic, if using, wine, lemon juice, thyme, sage, bay leaves, parsley sprigs and salt and pepper.
2 Pour in about 7 cups fresh cold water to cover. Bring to a boil, then lower the heat, cover and simmer gently for 30 minutes.
3 Meanwhile, melt the butter in a large saucepan, add the leeks, celery and chopped parsley and cook gently, stirring from time to time, for about 5 minutes. Season with salt and pepper. Pour in about 7 cups fresh cold water to cover. Bring to a boil, then lower the heat, cover and simmer very gently

for about 30 minutes, until the vegetables are tender but firm.
4 Meanwhile, pat the fish fillets dry with absorbent kitchen paper. Using a very sharp knife, cut them in 1-1½ inch pieces.
5 Strain and measure the fish stock and, if necessary, boil rapidly to reduce to 6 cups. Then, strain the vegetables and measure 6 cups of the stock. Pour both of the stocks into a very large saucepan or fish poacher (see Cook's tip) and add the cooked vegetables. Taste and adjust the seasoning.
6 Bring the contents of the pan to a boil, then lower the heat to the

very lowest simmering point. ⚠ Gently lower the fish pieces into the pan, cover and simmer for no longer than 5 minutes, until the fish is just cooked. ⚠ Remove at once from the heat.
7 In a warmed soup tureen or large bowl, combine the egg yolks with the ¼ cup light cream and the chives.
8 Thoroughly blend 1 ladle of hot soup with the egg yolk mixture then very carefully pour in the rest of the soup, making sure that the fish pieces do not break up. Serve at once in warmed soup bowls, with a spoonful of cream swirled on the top of each, if liked.

Cook's Notes

 TIME
Preparation takes about 25 minutes. Cooking the fish and vegetable stock takes about 30 minutes; finishing the soup, including cooking the fish, takes about 15 minutes.

BUYING GUIDE
Try to buy the fish from a good fishmarket and experiment with some of the more exotic types, combining the more expensive kinds with those that are less costly. Lingcod, fluke, perch and flounder, or Pacific sole, white sea bass and silver hake are good combinations. If you use frozen fish fillets or steaks, you will still need spare fish trimmings from a fishmarket for the stock.

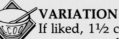 **VARIATION**
If liked, 1½ cups sliced carrots may be cooked with the leeks and celery, to make the dish more substantial and colorful.

 SERVING IDEAS
Serve the soup as a main course with hot French bread and butter, and accompany it with a dish of plain boiled potatoes, to make a complete and filling meal.

 **COOK'S TIP**
A fish poacher – a large, narrow pan with a tray or grid on which the fish is placed and then poached – is invaluable as the fish can be removed easily without any danger of disintegrating.

WATCHPOINTS
The stock must be at the very lowest simmering point – there should be barely a tremor on the surface – so that when the fish pieces are added they do not overcook or the soup will be ruined.
Watch the fish carefully once it is immersed, as it cooks extremely quickly.

●355 calories per portion

GERMANY

Sauerbraten (sour-sweet beef) is the German pot-roasted equivalent of a regular beef roast. Cooked in a very tasty spiced sauce, *Sauerbraten* is traditionally served with potato dumplings or buttered noodles and a dish of stewed apple.

Sauerbraten

SERVES 4
2 lb top round of beef, rolled and tied
¼ cup bacon drippings
3 tablespoons all-purpose flour
2 tablespoons butter
1 tablespoon light brown sugar
2 tablespoons seedless raisins (optional)

MARINADE
2 cups red wine
1¼ cups water
⅔ cup wine vinegar
1 large onion, thinly sliced
1 large carrot, thinly sliced
1 celery stalk, chopped
1 bay leaf
6 black whole peppercorns, crushed
3 allspice berries
3 cloves
1 teaspoon salt

1 Place the beef in a bowl large enough to contain it and also the marinade.
2 To make the marinade, put all the ingredients in a saucepan and bring slowly to a boil. Pour over the beef and let cool. Cover the bowl with plastic wrap and refrigerate for 3 days, turning the beef each day in the marinade.
3 Remove the beef from the marinade and pat dry with absorbent kitchen paper. Put the marinade in a saucepan and gently heat through.
4 Meanwhile, melt the bacon drippings in a Dutch oven, add the beef and sauté over moderate heat, turning to seal on all sides (see Cook's tips). Sprinkle the beef with 2 tablespoons of the flour and continue turning until it is completely browned all over.
5 Pour over half the marinade, lower the heat, cover and simmer for 1 hour. Pour over the remaining marinade and continue to cook for a further 30-60 minutes, or until the beef is tender and cooked through (the juices should run clear when the meat is pierced with a skewer).
6 Pour off the marinade into a bowl and let cool. Cover the pot and keep warm in the oven turned to lowest setting. Skim the fat from the surface of the cooled marinade, and then strain it (see Cook's tips).
7 Melt the butter in a small saucepan, sprinkle in the remaining flour and the sugar and stir over low heat for 1-2 minutes. Remove from heat and gradually stir in the skimmed marinade. Return to the heat and simmer, stirring, until thick and smooth. Remove from the heat. Stir in the raisins, if using. Return the sauce to the heat and reheat gently, stirring all the time.
8 Carve the beef into slices, then arrange overlapping on a warmed serving dish. Spoon over a little of the sauce. Serve with potato and bacon dumplings (see recipe) or buttered noodles and the remaining sauce passed separately in a warmed bowl.

Cook's Notes

Sauerbraten

 TIME
Preparing the *Sauerbraten* takes about 10 minutes. Allow 3 days marinating time. Cooking the dish takes about 2 hours.

 COOK'S TIPS
Use kitchen tongs to hold the beef roast securely as you turn it in the pot, so that the fat does not spit dangerously.
Reserve the beef fat skimmed from the marinade stock and store in the refrigerator for use as a delicious savory spread for toast.

VARIATION
For a creamy sauce, omit the raisins and stir ⅔ cup sour cream into the sauce at the end of stage 7. Reheat very gently but on no account let the sauce boil.

FREEZING
Freeze the sliced cooked beef in the sauce in a rigid container for up to 6 months. To serve: Thaw at room temperature for 3 hours, transfer to a saucepan and reheat gently, adding 1-2 tablespoons water to prevent the sauce from sticking. Stir gently when the meat slices can be separated. Heat through but do not allow to boil.

 SERVING IDEAS
Serve a light beer to drink with *Sauerbraten*, as the Germans do.
Pass a bowl of stewed apple spiced with cloves separately.

●585 calories per portion

Dumplings

TIME
Preparation, including boiling the potatoes, takes about 35 minutes. Cooking the dumplings takes about 15 minutes.

! WATCHPOINT
It is essential to keep the water boiling all the time, otherwise the dumplings may break up.

●100 calories each

Potato and bacon dumplings

MAKES 8

!

1 lb potatoes
salt
3 slices Canadian bacon, rinds removed, finely chopped
1 egg, beaten
1 cup soft white bread crumbs
2 teaspoons cornstarch
¼ teaspoon freshly grated nutmeg
vegetable oil, for greasing

1 Put the potatoes in a large saucepan of salted water. Bring to a boil and boil gently for 15-20 minutes.

2 Meanwhile brush the base of a large heavy-bottomed skillet with oil. Put the chopped bacon in the pan and sauté over moderate heat, stirring several times, for 3 minutes.

3 Bring a large saucepan of lightly salted water to a boil.

4 Drain the potatoes well and mash until smooth. Stir in egg, bread crumbs, cornstarch, ½ teaspoon salt, nutmeg and bacon. Mix then shape into dumplings (see Illustration).

5 Lower the dumplings into the boiling salted water and boil gently for 15 minutes. !

6 Using a slotted spoon, transfer the dumplings to a warmed serving dish and serve hot with the beef.

TO SHAPE DUMPLINGS

Cut round of dumpling mixture into 8 equal wedges. Shape each wedge into a ball, with well-floured hands.

The Black Forest region of south-west Germany is a famous cherry-growing area, and chocolate and cherry cakes have been popular there for over a hundred years. Black Forest torte, with its rich cream and cherry filling and Kirsch flavor is probably the most famous chocolate cake in the world. It makes an elegant and sophisticated dessert for any special occasion.

Black Forest torte

MAKES 8-10 SLICES
1¼ cups all-purpose flour
2 teaspoons baking soda
1 teaspoon coffee powder
1 tablespoon unsweetened cocoa
6 eggs, separated
⅔ cup superfine sugar
1 teaspoon lemon juice
3 squares (3 oz) semisweet chocolate, finely grated
pinch of salt
melted butter, for greasing
1 tablespoon each all-purpose flour and superfine sugar, for dusting

FILLING
2 lb Morello or Bing cherries (see Buying guide), pitted
½ cup granulated sugar
2½ cups water
⅔ cup Kirsch
2 cups heavy cream
3 tablespoons superfine sugar
1 square (1 oz) dark German chocolate, coarsely grated or flaked, for decoration

1 First prepare the cherries for the filling: Put the granulated sugar in a large, heavy-bottomed saucepan with the water. Heat gently until the sugar has dissolved, then bring to a boil and boil rapidly for 2 minutes without stirring. Remove from the heat and carefully add the cherries, then return to the heat and poach gently for 10 minutes.
2 Remove the cherries from the syrup with a slotted spoon and let cool. Boil the syrup rapidly for 2 minutes until thick. Off heat, measure ⅓ cup and let cool.
3 Preheat the oven to 350°F. Grease the base and sides of two 9 inch loose-bottomed cake pans with melted butter. Line the base of each pan with a round of waxed paper and grease the paper. Mix together the tablespoons of flour and sugar, sprinkle over the insides of the pans, then shake the pans until evenly coated. Shake off any excess.
4 To make the cakes: Sift the flour two or three times with the soda, coffee and cocoa powders.
5 In the top of a double boiler over simmering water, beat the egg yolks and sugar until thick enough to hold trail of beaters for 3 seconds when beaters are lifted. Mix in lemon juice and chocolate.
6 Put the egg whites and salt in a separate spotlessly clean and dry bowl. Beat together into soft peaks. Then stir 2 tablespoons of the beaten egg white into the egg yolk mixture. Using a large metal spoon, carefully fold a fourth of the remaining egg white into the mixture. Sift over 2 tablespoons of the flour mixture and carefully fold in. Repeat until all the egg white and the flour mixture have been added.
7 Divide batter equally between the pans and lightly smooth surface to break any large air bubbles.
8 Bake in the center of the oven, or just below for 25 minutes until the cakes are golden brown and the tops spring back when gently pressed. [!]

If you cannot get both pans on the same shelf, put one under the other and change them over midway through the cooking time.
9 Stand the pans on a wire rack for 10 minutes. Invert the cakes, remove paper, let cool completely.
10 Pat the cherries dry with absorbent kitchen paper and reserve 8 for decoration. Add ½ cup of the Kirsch to the reserved cherry syrup.
11 Beat the heavy cream to soft peaks and beat in the superfine sugar. Fold in the remaining Kirsch. Set aside 3-4 tablespoons of cream for decoration, if wished.
12 To assemble the cake: Split each sponge in 2 horizontally. Sprinkle one-third of the syrup over one bottom layer, cover with about one fourth of the cream and press half the fruit into the cream. Cover with a second sponge, sprinkle with more syrup, a layer of cream and the rest of the cherries. Lay the third sponge on top, sprinkle with the last of the syrup and cover with more whipped cream. Top with the last sponge layer and spread the remaining cream over the top and sides. Scatter grated chocolate over top and pipe rosettes of cream around the edge. Stud every other rosette with a cherry. Chill for 1 hour before serving.

Cook's Notes

TIME
Preparing cherries and sponge takes about 1 hour. Cooking takes 25 minutes; cooling 30 minutes. Allow 30 minutes for assembly and for chilling the torte 1 hour.

WATCHPOINT
Open the oven gently or the cakes will collapse in the draft.

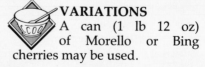

BUYING GUIDE
Buy Bing, sour or Morello cherries as the bright red cherries do not have enough flavor for this recipe.

VARIATIONS
A can (1 lb 12 oz) of Morello or Bing cherries may be used.

●670 calories per portion

Lebkuchen – spicy cookies – are just one of the famous range of German Christmas cookies, known collectively as *Weinachtsbäckerei* (literally, "Christmas baking"). *Lebkuchen* are traditionally eaten on St Nicolas Day (December 6) but improve in flavor and texture if stored in an airtight container, and may be served until Twelfth Night (January 6th).

Lebkuchen

MAKES ABOUT 60 COOKIES
4 cups finely ground almonds
⅓ cup candied peel, very finely chopped (see Buying guide)
2 teaspoons ground cinnamon
2 teaspoons ground cloves
2 teaspoons ground cardamom
6 eggs, separated
2 cups superfine sugar

GLAZE
finely grated rind of 1 lemon
1⅓ cups confectioners' sugar, sifted
¼ cup boiling water
red food coloring

TO DECORATE
multicolored sprinkles
chocolate sprinkles

1 Preheat the oven to 325°F.
2 Line two 13 × 12 inch baking sheets with rice paper or non-stick parchment (see Cook's tips).
3 Mix the finely ground almonds, candied peel and spices together in a bowl and set aside.
4 Put the egg yolks and sugar into a separate large mixing bowl. Using a hand-held electric beater, beat for about 10 minutes until the mixture is thick and cream-colored. Or use a rotary beater and beat the mixture for about 20 minutes or until mixture is thick.
5 In a separate clean, dry bowl, beat the egg whites until standing in stiff peaks. Take a large spoonful of the beaten egg whites and fold it into the yolk mixture, to loosen. Very gently fold in the remaining beaten egg whites.
6 Very gently fold the ground almond mixture into the egg and sugar mixture.
7 Place about 15 teaspoons of the mixture on each baking sheet, arranging the heaps as neatly as possible and spacing them out evenly, as the mixture will spread during baking.
8 Bake the cookies in the oven for about 15 minutes. They are ready when they are light brown and slightly soft to the touch. ⚠ Move the bottom sheet to the higher oven shelf when removing the top sheet and bake for a few minutes longer.

9 Let the baked cookies cool for a few minutes on the sheets, then transfer, with the lining paper, to a wire rack and let the cookies cool completely.
10 Repeat with the remaining mixture.
11 When the cookies are completely cold, break off the excess rice paper with your fingers; or peel off the non-stick parchment. Then make the glaze: Mix the grated lemon rind with the confectioners' sugar in a bowl. Very slowly add the boiling water, mix well with a fork. The glaze should be fairly runny.
12 Using a pastry brush, brush half the cookies with the glaze. Decorate with a few multicolored sprinkles as you finish each cookie.
13 When half the cookies have been covered with the white glaze, add 1-2 drops red coloring to the remaining glaze in the bowl, to color it pink. Use this to glaze the remaining cookies. Decorate with chocolate sprinkles as you finish each cookie.
14 Leave the cookies until the glaze has set completely, then store in an airtight tin until required or give as gifts (see Special Occasion).

Cook's Notes

 TIME
Preparation and baking take about 1 hour, decorating about 30 minutes.

 BUYING GUIDE
Try to buy real candied peel, available from specialist food stores.

 COOK'S TIPS
Rice paper, which can of course be eaten, is traditionally used for baking these cookies. The excess paper is broken off the cookies when they have cooled. In Germany where Lebkuchen are manufactured on a large commercial scale, they are often baked in special molds, but taste as good baked on sheets.

For correct consistency, do not skimp on beating time in stage 4.

⚠ WATCHPOINT
Watch the cookies carefully as they cook – they harden very quickly if baked too long.

SPECIAL OCCASION
It is well worth making a large quantity of Lebkuchen – not only because they disappear so rapidly, but they also make attractive and unusual Christmas presents. Line a small flat basket with pink paper and arrange the cookies in it. Cover with a piece of plastic wrap and decorate the basket with a pink satin ribbon bow.

● 55 calories per cookie

AUSTRIA

Crumbled veal scallops or *schnitzels*, sautéed until crisp and golden, are a famous specialty of Viennese (*Wiener*) cuisine. When cooked correctly they are not at all greasy; it used to be said that the test of a perfect *schnitzel* was that it should be dry enough to let a lady dressed in silk sit on it without marking her skirt!

Wiener schnitzel

SERVES 4
4 veal scallops, each weighing
   about 6 oz
2 tablespoons all-purpose flour
salt and freshly ground black pepper
1 egg
1 tablespoon milk
¾ cup fine dry white
   bread crumbs (see Cook's tips)
¼ cup butter
4 teaspoons vegetable oil
1 large lemon, cut in wedges

1 Preheat the oven to 225°F.
2 Place the veal scallops between 2 sheets of waxed paper and beat out until twice their original size (see Illustration).
3 Spread the flour out on a flat plate and season well with salt and pepper. Dip the scallops in the seasoned flour to coat them thoroughly.
4 Beat together the egg and milk in a shallow dish. Spread the bread crumbs out on a large, flat plate. Dip the floured scallops in the egg mixture, then in the bread crumbs to coat evenly all over.
5 Heat half the butter and half the oil in a large skillet over moderately high heat. Add 2 scallops and sauté briskly for 3 minutes on each side, until golden-brown and crisp. Drain on both sides on absorbent kitchen paper, then transfer to a warmed serving dish and keep warm in the oven while cooking the other 2 scallops.
6 Heat the remaining butter and oil, sauté the remaining scallops in the same way and drain on both sides on absorbent kitchen paper. Transfer to the serving dish, garnish with lemon wedges and serve at once.

PREPARING THE SCALLOPS

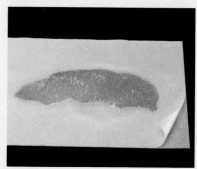

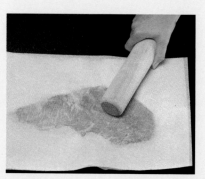

1 *On a board or working surface, place the scallop between 2 sheets of waxed paper, allowing plenty of room for the veal scallop to spread.*

2 *Beat with a rolling pin from center to each side, until the scallop has been flattened out smoothly and evenly to about twice its original size.*

Cook's Notes

 TIME
Preparation takes about 20 minutes, cooking about 15 minutes.

 COOK'S TIPS
It is best to make your own bread crumbs for this dish; stale leftover bread and crusts are ideal and, as a guide, 1 thick slice of bread makes about ¼ cup bread crumbs. Put the bread slices in the oven at the lowest possible setting and leave for several hours to dry out and harden. Then place in a plastic bag and crush with a rolling pin until fine. It is a good idea to make more crumbs than you need for this recipe. Store in a screwtop jar and use for rissoles, fish cakes and stuffings. White crumbs are best for this recipe but wholewheat crumbs are equally delicious for toppings or stuffings.

 SERVING IDEAS
Serve *Wiener schnitzels* with sauté potatoes and creamed spinach seasoned with freshly grated nutmeg.
In Vienna, a very light white wine such as Grinzinger (from the village of Grinzing outside Vienna) would accompany the schnitzels; this wine is always drunk in the year of its vintage (the year it is made, which is why it is referred to as a very "young" wine), and served chilled in earthenware pitchers. Grinzinger is not exported, so you can serve any well-chilled dry or medium white wine; an Austrian Schluck would make a good substitute or a German Liebfraumilch.
For Holstein schnitzel – top each cooked scallop with a fried egg and garnish with anchovies and a few capers.

●405 calories per portion

The Austrians are famous for their rich *torten* or cakes, and one of the best-known is Sachertorte; a moist, chocolate sponge cake glazed with jam, then covered with a thick, shiny chocolate icing. It was created by Franz Sacher, a master pastry-cook and founder of Vienna's famous Hotel Sacher.

Sachertorte

MAKES 12 SLICES

6 squares (6 oz) semisweet chocolate, broken in small pieces (see Buying guide)
2 tablespoons water
¾ cup butter, softened
1⅓ cups confectioners' sugar, sifted
6 large eggs, separated
2-3 drops vanilla
1¼ cups all-purpose flour, sifted
8 tablespoons apricot jam
melted butter, for greasing

ICING

5 squares (5 oz) semisweet chocolate, broken in small pieces
⅓ cup water
1 cup confectioners' sugar, sifted
2½ teaspoons glycerin (see Buying guide)

1 Preheat the oven to 350°F. Prepare a deep 9 inch round springform pan (see Illustration).
2 To make the cake: Put the chocolate and water in a small heat-proof bowl; place over a saucepan of gently simmering water and leave, stirring occasionally, until the chocolate has just melted. Remove the bowl from the pan. Set aside.
3 Meanwhile, in a large bowl, beat the butter until light and creamy. Add 1 cup confectioners' sugar, beat until pale and fluffy. Gradually beat in the egg yolks, then the melted chocolate and vanilla.
4 Beat the egg whites until they stand in soft peaks. Beat in the remaining confectioners' sugar and continue beating until the mixture is stiff.

Using a large metal spoon, lightly fold the beaten egg whites into the chocolate mixture, alternately with the flour. (Fold in about 2 tablespoons of flour at a time.)
5 Pour the batter into the prepared pan and make a shallow hollow in the center. Bake in the oven for 50-60 minutes, until a fine warmed skewer inserted in the center comes out clean.
6 Let the cake cool in the pan for 5 minutes, then invert it onto a wire rack. Carefully peel off the

lining paper; turn the cake the right way up and let cool for at least 2 hours, preferably overnight.
7 When you are ready to ice, cut the cold cake horizontally in half. (Use a sharp, long-bladed knife with a serrated edge and cut with a sawing action.) Next, strain the jam into a small saucepan; warm very gently until melted. Then remove from heat.
8 Place the top half of the cake, cut side uppermost, on a wire rack and spread with half the strained jam. Place the other half of the cake, cut

side down, on top. Spread the top and side with the rest of the jam.

9 Make the icing: Put the chocolate and water in a small heatproof bowl; place over a saucepan of gently simmering water and leave, stirring occasionally, until the chocolate has just melted. Remove from the heat and, using a balloon whip, whisk in confectioners' sugar and glycerin until the mixture is smooth.

10 Pour the icing over the cake and allow it to run down the side. If necessary, dip a spatula in hot water and use it to smooth the icing and give an even coating. Try to touch the icing as little as possible, to preserve the attractive gloss.

11 Leave the cake in a cool place for 2-3 hours until the icing has set. !

Cook's Notes

TIME
Preparing the cake batter takes about 40 minutes; baking about 1 hour, and cooling at least 2 hours (but preferably overnight). Icing, including preparing the icing, takes 30 minutes.

BUYING GUIDE
Buy a really good-quality chocolate to make this luxurious cake.

You can buy small bottles of glycerin from drugstores. It is used to prevent the icing from becoming brittle.

SERVING IDEAS
The Austrians like to eat Sachertorte with whipped cream.

Very much a special occasion cake, try making it for a birthday or other important family celebration.

WATCHPOINT
Do not be tempted to chill the cake in the refrigerator, as this will make the icing lose its gloss.

VARIATIONS
Try raspberry instead of apricot jam.

DID YOU KNOW
This cake is traditionally decorated with the word "Sacher" piped across the top when the icing has set.

●460 calories per slice

LINING THE CAKE PAN

1 *Stand pan on folded waxed paper. Outline base. Cut out 2 circles just inside the pencil outline.*

2 *Cut 2 thicknesses waxed paper strip 2 inches deeper than pan and long enough to overlap.*

3 *Make 1 inch fold along 1 long edge; unfold and snip diagonally at ½ inch intervals.*

4 *Grease pan. Place circle 1 in base. Arrange strip, snipped edge down. Put circle 2 on top. Grease.*

CZECHOSLOVAKIA

A fruity, spicy flavor is characteristic of many Czech dishes, and this delicious fish recipe is no exception. *Ryba na černo* literally means fish with black sauce – because of the prunes and raisins in the dish. In Czechoslovakia, which has no sea coast, a freshwater fish such as carp would be used, but trout, often more readily available, makes a very good substitute.

Ryba na černo

SERVES 4

4 rainbow trout or carp, each weighing about ¾ lb, cleaned but with heads and tails left on

COURT-BOUILLON (see Did you know)
2½ cups water
⅞ cup wine vinegar (see Buying guide)
2 onions, sliced
1 parsnip, diced
1 carrot, diced
1 celery stalk, chopped
1 small clove garlic, chopped
1 bay leaf
½ teaspoon whole cloves
½ teaspoon ground allspice
½ teaspoon ground ginger
salt and freshly ground black pepper
bay leaves, for garnish

SAUCE
1 cup pitted prunes, soaked if necessary, cooked for 10 minutes, then finely chopped (see Cook's tip)
⅓ cup seedless raisins
½ cup slivered almonds
¼ cup sugar
finely grated rind and juice of ½ lemon

1 Put all the ingredients for the *court-bouillon* into a large kettle or fish poacher. Bring to a boil and boil gently, covered, for 15 minutes.
2 Lower the trout carefully into the pan and turn down the heat. Cover and simmer gently for about 25 minutes, until the fish is just cooked (the flesh should flake easily when pierced with a sharp knife).
3 Meanwhile, combine the ingredients for the sauce in a large bowl. Preheat the oven to 225°F.

Cook's Notes

TIME
Preparation takes about 30 minutes, including cooking the prunes. Cooking takes about 45 minutes.

BUYING GUIDE
Either red or white wine vinegar gives the best flavor to the dish but malt vinegar may be used.

?

DID YOU KNOW
Court-bouillon is the French culinary term for the aromatic liquid in which fish, meat and vegetables are cooked. Use to add wonderful flavor to sauces.

●545 calories per portion

COOK'S TIP
Cook the prunes lightly; they should still be firm when chopped.

SERVING IDEAS
Serve with puréed potatoes, to soak up the sauce which is basically fairly thin, despite the chunks of fruit, because no thickening agent is used. Lightly cooked cabbage, tossed in butter and sprinkled with caraway seeds, is also delicious with this piquant fish dish.

Light beer is the best drink to accompany *Ryba na černo* – the sauce is too strongly flavored to go well with wine. Czech Pils would be ideal.

PREPARING FISH AND COURT-BOUILLON

1 *Using 2 fish turners, carefully remove the cooked trout from the large saucepan.*

2 *Pour the court-bouillon into a fine strainer and then let it drain into a bowl.*

4 Using 2 fish turners, carefully remove trout from pan (see Illustration). Place on a warmed large serving dish. Keep warm in the oven.
5 Strain *court-bouillon* (see Illustration). Mix thoroughly with the sauce ingredients in the bowl, then return to the rinsed-out pan.

6 Cook the sauce uncovered for 5 minutes, stirring occasionally, until heated through. Taste and adjust the seasoning, if necessary.
7 Spoon some of the sauce over the fish, garnish with bay leaves and serve at once, with the remaining sauce passed separately.

POLAND

Bigos, a slowly simmered stew of mixed game meats and sauerkraut (pickled cabbage), has been for centuries the most popular of Poland's national dishes, traditionally served on feast-days and holidays. The Poles are very fond of hunting, and in the old days a great cauldron of Bigos would hang all day over a wood fire in the forest, awaiting the return of the hungry huntsmen from the chase.

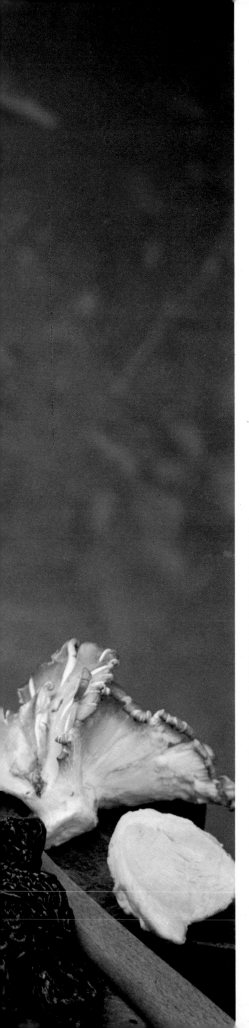

Bigos

SERVES 4

1¾ lb mixed cooked meats
  (e.g. pork, beef, veal, chicken,
  turkey or ham), cut in ¾ inch
  cubes and 1 inch matchsticks
  (see Cook's tips)
2 cans (1 lb size) sauerkraut,
  chopped, can juices reserved
2½ cups beef stock
2 tablespoons margarine or butter
2 large onions, sliced
¼ lb garlic sausage, skin
  removed and cut in ½ inch
  cubes
⅔ cup dried mushrooms (see
  Buying guide), soaked and cut
  in thin strips
20 dried prunes, soaked if
  necessary, pitted and chopped
2 bay leaves
pinch of ground allspice
salt and freshly ground black pepper
½ cup dry red wine

1 Put the sauerkraut with its juices into a 4 quart Dutch oven. Stir in the beef stock and add a little water if necessary just to cover. Set the pot over the lowest possible heat so that it is just simmering. Use a flame tamer if possible.

2 Melt the margarine in a skillet, add the onions and sauté gently for about 10 minutes until soft and brown. Remove the onions with a slotted spoon and stir into the sauerkraut.

3 Add the diced meats, garlic sausage, mushrooms, prunes, bay leaves and allspice to the pot and stir well. Season with salt and pepper.

4 Simmer the mixture over the lowest possible heat for 2½ hours so that the flavors blend.

5 Add the wine, taste and adjust seasoning if necessary, then stir well and simmer for a further 40 minutes until all the meats are very tender. Serve hot, straight from the pot or refrigerate and serve hot the following day (see Serving ideas).

Cook's Notes

TIME
Preparation takes about 30 minutes, cooking about 3 hours.

COOK'S TIPS
Cold cooked pheasant, duck or venison are traditionally included in Bigos, and make delicious additions if available. Some butchers and delicatessens sell smoked chicken, which would give an excellent flavor.

Cut the meats into both cube and matchstick lengths, for a varied texture.

BUYING GUIDE
Wild mushrooms grow profusely in the Polish countryside, and are traditionally strung onto long threads in the autumn and hung up to dry from the kitchen ceiling. These would be used for making Bigos in Poland, but in this country, you can use commercially dried mushrooms, available at most specialist (particularly Italian and oriental) food stores.

If you find them difficult to obtain, however, use 2 cups sliced button mushrooms sautéed in butter instead, and add about 1 hour before the end of cooking time. You could stir in a little mushroom ketchup as well, though nothing can replace the flavor of dried mushrooms.

SERVING IDEAS
Serve Bigos with rye, wholewheat or French bread. Beer or vodka is best to drink with Bigos, rather than wine.

Bigos is traditionally served on the third day after cooking, having first been brought to the simmering point and then allowed to cook for at least 1 hour on the 2 previous days. In between times it is stored in a cold place – ideally outdoors in a winter frost, which improves the flavor. Make Bigos at least the day before, if you can.

●615 calories per portion

The word *gefilte* is a Yiddish word, meaning "stuffed", and this dish probably originated among the Jewish population in Poland. The mixture of chopped fish, onions and other ingredients would have been served in a large filleted fish like carp or bream, but gradually it became popular to serve the ground fish mixture as individual balls. This is the way gefilte fish is served today, particularly at Passover and other similar Jewish celebrations.

Gefilte fish

MAKES 12-14 FISH BALLS
1 lb haddock (see Buying
    guide)
8-10 oz silver hake
½ lb halibut
10 oz herring
½ lb onions
1½ cups sliced carrots
salt and freshly ground black
    pepper
2½ cups cold water
2 eggs, lightly beaten
1⅓ cups medium matzo meal
    (see Buying guide)
¼ cup finely ground almonds
    (optional)
1 teaspoon sugar (optional)

1 Remove fish heads and tails and discard. Fillet and skin fish and put the bones and skin into the base of a large saucepan. Skin the onions and place the skin in the pan with the fish skin and bones.
2 Add sliced carrots, salt and black pepper. Pour on the water and bring to a boil. Lower heat and simmer, covered, for 30 minutes, then remove from heat. Put to one side in a warm place.
3 Grind or finely chop the fish and onions, using a grinder or food processor. [!] Place ground fish in a mixing bowl.
4 Add the eggs, matzo meal, finely ground almonds and sugar, if using. Season very generously and mix everything together thoroughly. Carefully roll the mixture into slightly flattish balls, about 2½ inches across (see Illustration).
5 Gently slide the balls into the liquid in the pan of fish stock. Return to the heat and cook, covered, on a low heat for 1 hour (see Cook's tip).
6 Leave the fish balls in the pan to cool and then remove carefully with a slotted spoon. Place the fish on a serving dish, overlapping them slightly . Arrange a piece of cooked carrot on top of each piece of fish.
7 Strain the cooking liquid into a pitcher. Put both the gefilte fish and the strained cooking liquid in the refrigerator and chill for 1 hour. Serve cold (see Serving ideas).

Cook's Notes

TIME
Preparation takes about 30 minutes. Cooking takes about 1½ hours. Allow at least 2 hours for cooling and chilling in the refrigerator.

BUYING GUIDE
This is a traditional gefilte fish mixture, a blend of haddock, silver hake, halibut and herring – a three to one proportion of dry white and rich oily fish. It is possible to substitute another fish mixture according to preference or availability. Lingcod and wolffish, for example, make a very good substitute for the haddock and hake. Or buy fillets and ask your supplier for some skin and bones to use in making the cooking stock.

You should be able to buy matzo meal at most delicatessens, but cracker meal can be used instead.

VARIATIONS
The same mixture can be used to make sautéed fish balls, which are a popular alternative to boiled ones; sauté the balls in hot shallow oil for about 7 minutes on each side, until they are quite brown. Or make much small balls and deep-fry them in oil. These make excellent cocktail snacks, served on sticks with a sweet and sour or homemade tomato dipping sauce.

COOK'S TIP
Check liquid during cooking time and, if necessary, add a little more water to prevent pan burning.

ECONOMY
As there are no fixed rules about which fish to use for this dish, ask your supplier to suggest a flavorsome but inexpensive selection.

DID YOU KNOW
Matzo meal is made from matzos, the crisp unleavened crackers which are eaten at Passover.

SERVING IDEAS
Boiled gefilte fish is almost always served cold, accompanied by its own sauce and by a special, very hot piquant sauce known as *chrane*, a horseradish and beet relish available ready-made in jars from Jewish delicatessens.

Fried gefilte fish is good hot or cold, served either with *chrane*, or mayonnaise.

Serve either boiled or fried gefilte as an appetizer, or as a main course with salads.

WATCHPOINT
Do not grind fish too fine – an electric food processor can reduce fish to a purée if you are not careful.

●135 calories per fish ball

SHAPING THE FISH BALLS

1 Add more matzo meal if the mixture is too liquid to make into firm balls. Stir well to mix.

2 Using slightly wet hands, roll the mixture into 12-14 flattened balls, 2½ inches across.

HUNGARY

A *paprikas* (pronounced "paprikash") is a very popular Hungarian dish made with pork, veal, lamb or chicken, mild paprika and lots of sour cream. *Paprikas* is traditionally served with dumplings called *nockerln,* and together they make a tasty meal.

Pork paprikas

SERVES 4-6

2 lb stew, pork, trimmed of excess fat and cut in ¾ inch cubes (see Buying guide)
2 tablespoons shortening or vegetable oil
1 lb onions, sliced
1 clove garlic, minced (optional)
1 tablespoon mild paprika
salt
⅔ cup water
1 green pepper, seeded and sliced
1 sweet red pepper, seeded and sliced
½ lb tomatoes, peeled and sliced
1¼ cups sour cream

1 Melt the shortening in a large, heavy-bottomed saucepan or Dutch oven. Add the onions and garlic, if using, and sauté gently for 5-10 minutes, until the onions are soft and lightly colored. Remove with a slotted spoon and drain on absorbent kitchen paper.
2 Stir in the paprika and cook gently for 1 minute. [!]
3 Add about one-fourth of the pork cubes to the pan and cook quickly, stirring, over moderate heat until lightly colored. Remove the pork from the pan, set aside with the onions and cook the remaining pork cubes in the same way, in 3 more batches.
4 Return the pork and onions to the pan. Season to taste with salt, add the water and bring to a boil. Lower the heat, cover the pan tightly and simmer for 1 hour.
5 Add the peppers and tomatoes to the pan and simmer for a further 30 minutes. [✳]
6 Beat the sour cream with a fork until smooth. Reserve about ½ cup and stir remainder into the pan (see Cook's tip). Heat gently, stirring, but do not let boil or the cream will separate. Taste and adjust seasoning and serve at once with the reserved cream swirled on top or passed separately in a pitcher. Accompany the pork paprikas with a dish of hot nockerln.

Nockerln

SERVES 4-6

2 cups all-purpose flour   [!]
salt and freshly ground black pepper
¾ cup carbonated water (see Cook's tip)
2 tablespoons butter, to finish

1 Sift the flour into a large bowl and season with plenty of salt and pepper. Bring a large saucepan of salted water to a boil.
2 Very gradually add the carbonated water to the flour, mixing with a fork until the dough is a soft but not sticky consistency.
3 Drop teaspoonfuls of the dough into the boiling water (see Illustration). When the dumplings rise to the surface, cook for about 5 minutes. [!] Drain the dumplings thoroughly in a colander.

4 Melt the butter in a saucepan. Add the drained dumplings and carefully turn them to coat with the butter.
5 Pile the dumplings into a warmed serving dish and serve with the pork paprikas.

COOKING NOCKERLN

Drop a teaspoonful of the dough into the boiling water, immersing the spoon to make scooping up of the next portion of dough easier.

Cook's Notes

Pork paprikas

 TIME
Preparing the Pork paprikas takes about 10 minutes, and cooking this dish takes about 1 hour 35 minutes, plus 5 minutes to finish.

BUYING GUIDE
Thick end of belly, which has a higher proportion of lean meat to fat than the flank end, is a good cut for this dish. Belly of pork gives a very tender result and is considerably less expensive then either shoulder butt or tenderloin of pork.

COOK'S TIP
Always beat sour cream before adding to a hot dish, as this helps to give a smoother finish.

WATCHPOINT
It is important to heat the paprika to release its full flavor, but do be sure to keep the heat low as it will burn easily if overheated at this stage.

 FREEZING
The paprikas freezes well without the cream. Prepare to the end of stage 5, transfer to a rigid container, cool quickly, then seal, label and freeze for up to 3 months. To serve: Thaw at room temperature, then gently heat through on top of the range until bubbling. Finish as in stage 6.

●530 calories per portion

Nockerln

TIME
The nockerln take about 15 minutes to prepare and cook.

COOK'S TIP
Using carbonated water helps to make the dumplings lighter.

 WATCHPOINT
Do not overcook the dumplings or they will harden.

●250 calories per portion

ITALY

Veal is Italy's favorite meat, and there is a vast range of Italian veal recipes. *Osso buco*, braised veal shank, is especially popular; the marrow in the center of the bones is considered a great delicacy. *Osso buco*, which originated in Lombardy in northern Italy, is one of Italy's great classic dishes, but it is particularly associated with Milan where it is traditionally served with *Risotto alla Milanese* – rice cooked with dry white wine, chicken stock and butter and sprinkled with Parmesan cheese.

Osso buco

SERVES 4
4 slices veal shank, about
   2½ inches thick and each
   weighing about 10 oz (see
   Buying guide)
2 tablespoons all-purpose flour
salt and freshly ground black pepper
¼ cup butter
2 tablespoons olive oil
1 onion, minced
1 small carrot, finely chopped
1 celery stalk, finely chopped
⅔ cup dry white wine
1 can (16 oz) tomatoes
2 tablespoons tomato paste
1 bay leaf
¼ teaspoon dried sage
¼ teaspoon sugar

TO FINISH
1 glove garlic, minced
finely grated rind of ½ lemon
2 tablespoons finely chopped fresh
   parsley

1 Firmly tie each piece of veal in 2 places with thin twine so that it will keep in a neat shape during cooking. Spread the flour out on a flat plate, season with salt and pepper and turn the veal in the seasoned flour, to coat thoroughly.
2 Heat half the butter and oil in a large shallow flameproof casserole, add the veal and sauté quickly, turning it until browned all over. Drain the veal well over the casserole, then transfer to a large plate and set aside.
3 Heat the remaining butter and oil in the casserole, add the onion, carrot

and celery and sauté gently for 5 minutes, stirring occasionally, until onion is soft and lightly colored.
4 Pour the wine into the casserole and simmer, uncovered, for 8-10 minutes until reduced by half. Stir in the tomatoes with their juice and the tomato paste. Add the bay leaf, sage and sugar. Stir well and season with salt and pepper. Bring slowly to a boil, stirring constantly.
5 Return the veal to the casserole, making sure that the bones are upright, to prevent the marrow from falling out during cooking. Cover closely with a lid and simmer gently for 1½-2 hours or until the veal is very tender (the meat should be almost falling from the bones).
6 Meanwhile, mix finishing ingredients together in a small bowl.
7 Sprinkle finishing mixture over the veal 3-4 minutes before serving and spoon the sauce over the veal, keeping veal upright, to distribute the flavor. Remove twine and serve hot, straight from the casserole (see Serving ideas).

Cook's Notes

 TIME
Preparation takes about 30 minutes, cooking about 2 hours.

 BUYING GUIDE
Order the veal shank well in advance from the butcher. Slices are cut across the leg and should be as meaty as possible, and must include the bone complete with the marrow in the center.

 SERVING IDEAS
Serve with risotto or buttered noodles.

 DID YOU KNOW
The finish of garlic, lemon rind and parsley gives *osso buco* its essential Milanese touch. The finish is called *gremolata* in Italian.
   In Italy, some restaurants provide a special marrow fork or spoon to scoop out every last bit of marrow from the center of the bones.

●450 calories per portion

SPAIN

Paella, a wonderfully tasty mixture of saffron rice, meat, fish and vegetables, must be Spain's most famous dish. You can ring endless changes on the ingredients; the recipe given here – using chicken, pork, spicy sausage and shellfish – is just one version.

The only essential ingredients for every paella are long-grain rice, olive oil and saffron.

The beauty of paella is that it can be simple or elaborate, and the ingredients varied to suit your pocket as well as your taste.

You can serve it for a simple summer lunch, or dress it up as a more elaborate, but easy-to-prepare party dish. Paella is perfect for a buffet, as it can so easily be eaten with a fork.

Paella

SERVES 6

12 unshucked mussels, thawed if frozen (see Illustration), or 1 can or jar (5 oz) mussels, drained
2 lb chicken, cut in 8 pieces
¼ lb lean pork tenderloin, cut in ½ inch cubes
salt and freshly ground black pepper
7 tablespoons olive oil
2 raw chorizo sausages, cut in ¼ inch slices
1 onion, minced
2 cloves garlic, minced (optional)
1 sweet red pepper, seeded and cut in 1½ × ¼ inch strips
½ lb tomatoes, peeled, seeded and finely chopped
1 teaspoon mild paprika
2⅓ cups long-grain rice
½ teaspoon saffron strands, crushed and soaked for 2 hours in 4 cups boiling chicken stock
1½ cups cooked shrimp in shells, thawed if frozen (see Buying guide), or ⅔ cup shelled shrimp, thawed if frozen, or 1 can (about 8 oz) shelled shrimp, drained
1 can (16 oz) artichoke hearts, drained
1½ cups frozen peas, thawed

1 If using unshucked mussels, prepare them as shown in the Illustration.
2 Cook the prepared mussels: Rinse the soaked mussels thoroughly, then drain. Pour ⅓ cup water into a heavy skillet large enough to hold the mussels in a single layer. Add the mussels, cover and bring to a boil then lower the heat and simmer for 5-6 minutes, shaking the pan gently once or twice. If the mussels have not opened cook for 1-2 minutes longer. Discard any unopened mussels !| and set the rest aside.
3 Season the chicken pieces and pork cubes with salt and pepper. Heat half the oil in a paella pan (see Did you know), large skillet, or large, shallow flameproof casserole. Add the chicken and pork and sauté over moderate heat for 10-15 minutes, turning frequently, until brown on all sides. After 5 minutes cooking, add the sausage slices to the pan and turn to brown. With a slotted spoon, lift out the meats onto a plate and set aside.
4 Heat the remaining oil in the pan. Add the onion, garlic, if using, pepper strips and chopped tomatoes and cook over gentle heat for about 5 minutes, stirring from time to time, until the onion is soft and the mixture well blended. Stir in the paprika. Cook for 1 minute. Remove from heat. Stir in rice.
5 Strain the saffron stock into the pan and stir once. Bring to a boil and cook for 5 minutes.
6 Arrange the chicken, pork, sausages, cooked mussels, shrimp and artichoke hearts on top of the rice. Sprinkle over the peas.
7 Turn down heat to low. Cook for 12-15 minutes, until rice is tender and all liquid absorbed.
8 Turn off the heat under the pan. Cover the pan with a lid or drape it with a dish towel. Leave for 3-4 minutes, to allow the flavors to blend. Serve straight from the pan.

TO CLEAN MUSSELS

1 *Check mussels are really fresh: Tap any open ones against working surface. Discard if they do not shut.*

2 *Pull away any beards (pieces of hanging seaweed gripped between the 2 shells of the mussel).*

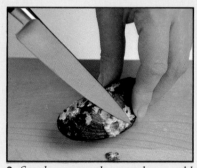

3 *Scrub mussels under cold running water, then scrape away encrustations with a sharp knife. Then soak mussels in fresh cold water to cover for 2-3 hours. Change the water several times.*

Cook's Notes

TIME
Preparation takes about 1¼ hours if using un-shucked mussels. Allow a further 2-3 hours for soaking the mussels and saffron threads. Cooking the paella takes about 45 minutes.

WATCHPOINT
It is absolutely vital to discard any unopened mussels – this shows they are not fresh, which can cause serious food poisoning.

BUYING GUIDE
Try to buy mussels and shrimp in the shell, as they look so attractive in the finished dish. Both are available from good fishmarkets, and frozen from some super-markets.

SERVING IDEAS
Serve the paella at the table straight from the pan, as the Spaniards do.

The paella is usually eaten by itself – a vegetable accompaniment is not necessary.

VARIATIONS
In Spain, paella is often made with rabbit, and this could be substituted for chicken.

For a special occasion, add some lobster meat to the paella.

DID YOU KNOW
The name paella comes from *paellera*, the pan in which the dish is traditionally cooked in Spain; it is shallow with gently sloping sides and 2 flattened handles. You can buy special paella pans from high-quality kitchen equipment stores or departments of big stores – or, better still, buy one on holiday in Spain. But if you do not have a *paellera*, a large heavy skillet, preferably with a lid, or a large, shallow flame-proof casserole will do very well instead for making the paella.

●980 calories per portion

This is a very old traditional dish from southern Spain, typical of Andalusia and La Mancha. There are many regional variations, some with very little liquid and some without tomatoes; olive oil and red wine vinegar, however, are always included.

Originally a midday meal, gazpacho was prepared on the spot in a wooden bowl and eaten with wooden spoons by workers in the fields. This sophisticated modern version makes a wonderfully refreshing cold vegetable soup in summer, when cucumbers, tomatoes and green peppers are at their best. The soup is served in individual bowls with garnishes of croutons, hard-cooked eggs, cucumbers, peppers and onion.

Gazpacho

SERVES 4

1 lb tomatoes, peeled and
    roughly chopped
½ cucumber, pared and
    roughly chopped
1 green pepper, seeded and
    roughly chopped
1 small onion, roughly chopped
1 clove garlic, chopped
2 slices white bread, crusts
    removed, crumbled
1 teaspoon salt, or to taste
2 tablespoons red wine vinegar
4 cups ice water
⅓ cup olive oil

TO SERVE

2 slices bread, crusts removed,
    cubed
¼ cup olive oil
2 eggs, hard-cooked and chopped
½ cucumber, pared and finely
    chopped
1 small green pepper, seeded and
    finely chopped
1 onion, finely diced (see Illustration)

1 In a large bowl, combine the tomatoes, cucumber, green pepper, onion, garlic, bread, salt and vinegar. Add the water and mix thoroughly (see Cook's tip). Purée the mixture in a food processor or blender until smooth. Return the purée to the bowl and beat in the oil in a thin, steady stream. Cover the bowl with plastic wrap and refrigerate for about 2 hours until thoroughly chilled.
2 To make the croutons: Heat the oil in a heavy skillet over moderate heat until very hot, add the bread cubes and sauté until golden brown on all sides, turning them frequently. Drain on absorbent kitchen paper and put into a small serving bowl.
3 Put the eggs, cucumber, green pepper and onion into separate small serving bowls.
4 When the soup is well chilled, stir thoroughly $\boxed{!}$ and taste and adjust seasoning. Pour into 4 chilled individual soup bowls and pass the garnishes separately.

Cook's Notes

 TIME
Preparation takes about 45 minutes, but remember that the soup needs to be chilled for about 2 hours.

 WATCHPOINT
Do not forget to stir the soup just before serving.

COOK'S TIP
If the tomatoes have a poor color, add some tomato paste to the ingredients before you purée them.

● 370 calories per portion

HOW TO DICE ONIONS

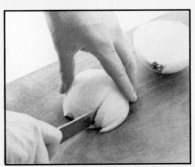

1 *Peel the onion and cut it in half lengthwise with a sharp knife on a chopping board.*

2 *Place the onion with the cut side down. Slice the onion horizontally, leaving the root end uncut.*

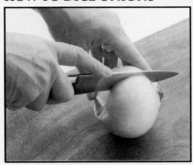

3 *Cut the onion lengthwise, again leaving the root end uncut.*

4 *Now cut across the onion, which will fall into tiny dice.*

Tortilla española or *tortilla de patatas,* the famous Spanish omelet made with sautéed potatoes and onions, is quite different from a French folded omelet, because it is flat and is cooked on both sides for considerably longer. In Spain it's usually served hot or cold as an appetizer, and is also eaten cold as a snack, cut in cubes. As a lunch or supper main course, it may be accompanied by slices of spicy sausage and a fresh tomato sauce.

Tortilla española

SERVES 2-4

4 large eggs, beaten
¼ cup olive oil (see Cook's tips)
1½ cups finely chopped onions
¾ lb potatoes cut in ½ inch dice (see Buying guide)
salt and freshly ground black pepper
olives and sweet pepper rings, for garnish (optional)

1 Heat 3 tablespoons of the oil in a large, heavy-bottomed skillet (see Cook's tips). Add onions and potatoes, cover the pan and cook over moderate heat, stirring occasionally, for about 15 minutes, until the onions and potatoes are soft and golden. ☐

2 Remove the vegetables from the pan with a slotted spoon, transfer to a large plate and let cool for 5 minutes.

3 Wipe out the pan thoroughly with several sheets of absorbent kitchen paper.

4 Season the beaten eggs with salt and pepper and gently stir in the cooled onions and potatoes into the egg mixture.

5 Heat the remaining oil in the pan, add the egg and vegetable mixture and cook, uncovered, over moderate heat for 12-15 minutes until the base is set but the center of the omelet is still slightly creamy.

6 Run a spatula around the edge of the omelet and remove the pan from the heat. Invert a large round plate over the pan (see Cook's tips and Illustrations), then holding the pan and plate firmly together, invert the pan and carefully turn the omelet onto the plate.

HOW TO TURN THE OMELET

1 *Invert plate over pan, then holding pan and plate together, invert pan and turn omelet onto plate.*

2 *Carefully slip the omelet back into the pan, browned side uppermost. Allow base to brown.*

7 Carefully slip the omelet back into the pan (see Illustration), browned side uppermost. Cook over moderate heat for a further 3-5 minutes, until the underside is browned.

8 Slide the omelet onto a warmed round serving platter and garnish with olives and sweet pepper rings, if liked. Serve the omelet cut in wedges (see Serving ideas).

GREECE

Moussaka, a spicy dish of ground meat, eggplants and tomatoes baked with a delicious savory topping, is one of the most popular main-course choices in Greek homes and restaurants. In fact, there are few better ways of conjuring up the atmosphere of a Greek taverna than by serving Moussaka with salad and a bottle of Greek wine.

Moussaka

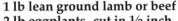

SERVES 6

1 lb lean ground lamb or beef
2 lb eggplants, cut in ½ inch slices
salt
about 1 cup sunflower-seed oil (see Watchpoints)
1 lb onions, thinly sliced
2 cloves garlic, cut in slivers
1½ lb tomatoes, peeled and sliced
2 tablespoons beef stock
½ teaspoon dried basil
freshly ground black pepper
½ lb Gruyère or Cheddar cheese, thinly sliced
2 tablespoons chopped parsley

TOPPING
1 tablespoon butter
2 tablespoons all-purpose flour
1¼ cups milk
2 eggs, separated
pinch of freshly grated nutmeg

1 Put the sliced eggplants in a colander and sprinkle them with salt, turning to coat evenly. Set the colander on a plate and leave to drain for 30 minutes.

2 Heat about ¼ cup oil in a large, heavy-bottomed skillet. Add the onions and garlic and sauté over moderate heat, stirring occasionally for about 15 minutes, until golden. Remove from the pan with a slotted spoon, drain on absorbent kitchen paper and set aside.

3 Heat a further 2 tablespoons oil in the pan. Add the ground lamb and fry gently, stirring often to remove any lumps, for 5-10 minutes until the meat has lost all its pinkness. Remove the meat from the pan with a slotted spoon, drain on absorbent kitchen paper and set aside with the onions.

4 Rinse the eggplants under cold running water and pat dry with absorbent kitchen paper.

5 Heat a further ¼ cup oil in the pan, add the eggplants and sauté over moderate heat, turning occasionally, for 10-15 minutes until golden on both sides. Add more oil as necessary. Drain the sautéed eggplant thoroughly on absorbent kitchen paper. !

6 Meanwhile, put the tomatoes in a saucepan, add the beef stock and basil and season with salt and pepper. Cook over gentle heat, stirring occasionally with a wooden spoon for 10-15 minutes, to make a thick, pulpy and richly flavored sauce.

7 Preheat the oven to 350°F.

8 Brush a 12 × 8 × 2 inch baking dish with oil. In the dish, make layers of eggplants, cheese, ground lamb and onions, seasoning the layers with salt and pepper and moistening with the tomato sauce. Repeat until all the ingredients are used.

9 Make the topping: Melt the butter in a saucepan, sprinkle in the flour and stir over low heat until straw-colored. Off heat, gradually stir in the milk. Return to the heat and simmer, stirring, until thickened and smooth. Remove from heat and let cool slightly. Beat in the egg yolks and a pinch of nutmeg. Beat the egg whites until soft peaks form, then fold lightly but thoroughly into the sauce mixture.

10 Pour the topping over the dish and bake in the oven for about 1 hour, until the topping is browned. Remove from oven and sprinkle with the parsley. Serve hot, straight from the dish.

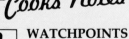

Cook's Notes

TIME
Preparation, including precooking and draining the eggplants, takes about 1 hour; cooking, 1 hour.

SERVING IDEAS
Accompany moussaka with a salad and a loaf of Greek bread, with Greek pastries to follow.
Serve with a popular Greek wine such as *retsina*, or a full-bodied red.

WATCHPOINTS
Eggplants soak up oil like blotting paper, so have extra ready to add to the pan if it shows signs of becoming dry.
Draining on absorbent kitchen paper is essential, otherwise the finished dish will be too oily.

VARIATIONS
Mint or coriander may be used instead of basil, and allspice is often used in place of the grated nutmeg.
Thinly sliced, lightly sautéed potatoes may be added with the eggplants or zucchini may be substituted for eggplants.
In Greece, plain yogurt is often used to thicken the topping mixture, or it may be flavored with Greek cheese, such as shredded Haloumi. In this case, omit the other cheese from the layers.

● 800 calories per portion

Lamb is the most popular meat in Greece, where the hilly countryside is better suited to grazing sheep than cattle. The Greeks cook lamb in a variety of ways – roasted on a spit or grilled over charcoal. Here the succulent, tender meat is cooked on top of the range and served in a tangy egg and lemon sauce.

Accompanied by a simple pilaf of rice and a salad of lettuce and tomato, Avgolemono lamb is a great favorite with Greek families. Try it for a summer meal, and bring some of the atmosphere of a sunny Greek island to your table. To drink with the lamb, serve chilled Retsina, the Greek white wine with pine resin added, which gives it a distinctive smoky taste. Retsina is now widely available.

Avgolemono lamb

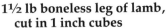

SERVES 4
1½ lb boneless leg of lamb,
   cut in 1 inch cubes
2 tablespoons margarine or butter
1 large onion, chopped
4 celery stalks, chopped
1 tablespoon chopped fresh dill or
   1 teaspoon dried dillweed
2½ cups vegetable or light
   chicken stock
salt and freshly ground black pepper
2 small firm hearts of round lettuce,
   cut in quarters (see Cook's tips)
4 teaspoons cornstarch
2 egg yolks
2 tablespoons lemon juice
2 tablespoons chopped parsley
lemon wedges, for garnish

1 Melt the margarine in a large heavy-bottomed saucepan. Add the onion and cook gently for about 5 minutes until soft and lightly colored. Add the lamb, increase heat and stir until meat is sealed but not browned (see Cook's tips).
2 Add the celery, the dill and stock to the pan and season to taste with salt and pepper. Bring to a boil, cover, lower heat and simmer for 1 hour. ✳
3 Preheat oven to 225°F.

4 Put the lettuce in a colander, pour over boiling water and drain well. Add the lettuce to the pan, cover and simmer for 15 minutes.
5 Strain off the cooking liquid from the lamb into a clean saucepan. Keep the meat and vegetables warm in the oven.
6 To make the sauce: In a small bowl, mix the cornstarch to a smooth paste with a little water. Heat the cooking liquid in the saucepan and when boiling add the cornstarch paste and cook over moderate heat, stirring constantly, until the sauce is thick and smooth. Lower the heat and simmer for 2 minutes.
7 Meanwhile, beat the egg yolks in a large bowl until creamy. Beat in the lemon juice, a little at a time, until it is all incorporated. Gradually stir the hot sauce into the egg and lemon mixture in the bowl, [!] beating well until thoroughly blended. Return to the pan and reheat gently, stirring, without allowing it to boil. Taste and adjust the seasoning, if necessary.
8 Arrange the lamb and vegetables on a warmed serving dish and pour over the sauce. Sprinkle with the parsley, garnish with the lemon wedges and serve at once.

Greek pilaf

SERVES 4
¼ cup margarine or butter
1 onion, finely chopped
1 cup long-grain rice
2¼ cups chicken stock
⅓ cup pitted ripe olives,
   chopped

[!]

1 Melt the margarine in a saucepan, add the onion and sauté gently until soft but not colored. Add the rice

and stir gently over moderate heat for 2 minutes, until the grains are thoroughly coated. [!] Pour in the stock, stir to mix and bring to a boil. Stir once, cover and simmer gently for about 20 minutes, or until the rice is tender and fluffy and all the stock is absorbed. [!]
2 Fork in the chopped olives, cover pan and leave for 3 minutes. Serve at once (see Serving ideas).

Cook's Notes

Avgolemono lamb

 TIME
Preparation takes about 20 minutes. Cooking takes about 1½ hours.

 COOK'S TIPS
Use the outer lettuce leaves to make a salad to accompany the dish.
"Sealing" the meat ensures that the flavor and juices do not escape during cooking.

 SERVING IDEAS
Serve the dish with Greek pilaf (see recipe), pita bread, and a salad of shredded lettuce and sliced tomatoes and onion.

 WATCHPOINT
It is important to add the hot sauce gradually to the uncooked beaten egg yolks, beating all the time, and to reheat very gently to avoid curdling.

✳ FREEZING
Prepare the recipe up to the end of stage 2. Transfer to a rigid container, cool, seal and label. Freeze for up to 6 months. To serve: Transfer to a large saucepan and reheat gently from frozen on top of the range, until heated right through. Complete from stage 3.

●520 calories per portion

Greek pilaf

 TIME
Preparation and pre-cooking 5 minutes, simmering rice, 20 minutes.

 SERVING IDEAS
Press the cooked pilaf into an oiled 4 cup mold, or into individual molds or custard cups, then invert onto a serving dish.

! WATCHPOINTS
Stir rice very gently to avoid it being sticky.
Do not uncover or stir during cooking, or rice will dry out.

●270 calories per portion

TURKEY

Imam bayildi, a Turkish dish of fragrantly stuffed eggplants, means literally "the priest fainted", the legend being that a certain *imam* or priest overdid the helpings and promptly passed out from a surfeit of pleasure. Other versions say that the *imam* fainted when he heard the cost of the dish because of the amount of oil used in making it. Traditionally, olive oil is used, but for the sake of economy, we have substituted sunflower-seed oil.

Imam bayildi is a delicious appetizer which is eaten cold. Although it can be served the same day it is made, the flavor improves considerably if the dish is left overnight.

Imam bayildi is quite filling, so serve a light main course to follow.

Imam bayildi

SERVES 6

4 eggplants, each weighing about 6 oz (see Buying guide)
salt
⅔-1¼ cups sunflower-seed oil (see Watchpoint)
1 lb onions, finely chopped
4 cloves garlic, finely sliced
⅓ cup dried currants
freshly ground black pepper
pinch of ground allspice
1½ lb large tomatoes, peeled and chopped (see Buying guide)
bunch of fresh parsley, finely chopped
3-4 bay leaves
sprig of fresh thyme, or ½ teaspoon dried thyme
lettuce leaves or coriander, and lemon wedges, for garnish (optional)

1 Wipe the eggplants with a damp cloth and trim off the stems. Cut each eggplant in half lengthwise, then score the flesh with a knife and sprinkle with salt (see Illustration).
2 Put the eggplants, cut side up, in a colander, cover with a plate and weight down with a 4½ lb weight (see Cook's tip). Leave for 2 hours to draw out the bitter juices.

HOW TO PREPARE EGGPLANTS

1 *Wipe the eggplants with a damp cloth. Then, using a sharp knife, trim off the stems and cut each eggplant in half lengthwise. Score the flesh of the eggplant and sprinkle it evenly all over with salt.*

2 *Put the eggplants in a colander, cut side up, and set over a saucepan. Cover with a plate and weight down with a 4½ lb weight or with flour or sugar bags or cans. Leave the eggplants for 2 hours to draw out the bitter juices.*

3 Rinse the eggplants under cold running water and pat dry with absorbent kitchen paper. Then, using a small knife, scoop out the flesh, taking care not to damage the skin.
4 Heat ⅔ cup oil in a large skillet, add the onions and garlic and sauté gently for 5 minutes until the onions are soft and lightly colored.
5 Meanwhile, put the dried currants in a bowl and cover with boiling water. Leave to swell for 1-2 minutes.
6 Add the eggplant flesh to the skillet, with salt and pepper to taste. Drain the dried currants, if necessary, then stir into the eggplant mixture with the allspice.
7 Add the chopped tomato flesh and parsley to the eggplant mixture, stir well to mix, then cook for 10-15 minutes, stirring constantly. Add more oil if the mixture becomes dry.

8 Meanwhile, preheat the oven to 325°F.
9 Remove the mixture from the heat, taste and adjust seasoning.
10 Put the eggplant shells close together in an ovenproof dish and spoon in the cooked stuffing. Any surplus mixture can be pressed in alongside the shells. Crumble the bay leaves over the top and sprinkle over the thyme.
11 Bake in the oven for about 1¼ hours or until the eggplant shells are cooked and look translucent.
12 Let cool in the oil, then cover and refrigerate overnight, still in the oil.
13 Remove the dish from the refrigerator 2 hours before serving to take the chill off. Serve cold, arranged on a serving platter, garnished with lettuce or coriander and lemon wedges, if liked. Serve any extra stuffing in a bowl.

Cook's Notes

 TIME
For best results make *imam bayildi* the day before it is needed and allow for cooling and overnight chilling in the refrigerator. Draining the eggplants takes 2 hours, preparation 40 minutes and cooking about 1¼ hours.

WATCHPOINT
Eggplants have an infinite capacity for absorbing oil, so make sure you have more oil handy in case.
The juice stains so avoid contact with your clothes.

 BUYING GUIDE
You will need long eggplants rather than the more rounded ones.
Beefsteak tomatoes are particularly good in this recipe because they have more flavor.

 COOK'S TIP
If you do not have kitchen scale weights, use bags of flour or sugar or some heavy cans to weight down the eggplants.

SERVING IDEAS
Serve with hot pita bread for scooping up the filling.

●375 calories per portion

ISRAEL

Falafel – small, spicy rissoles made from chick-peas – have been adopted as one of Israel's favorite national dishes, although in fact they originated in Egypt as *ta'amia*, patties made from dried white beans. Falafel are eaten on many occasions – as a snack dipped into plain yogurt or hummus, for lunch with a variety of salads, or even for breakfast. They are sold in cafés and by street vendors as an Israeli version of "fast food", and may be tucked into a pocket of pita bread for easy eating.

Falafel

MAKES ABOUT 20
1¼ cups dried chick-peas, soaked overnight (see Buying guide)
1 large onion, minced
4 tablespoons fresh parsley, finely chopped
1 clove garlic, crushed
1 teaspoon ground coriander
1 teaspoon ground cumin
good pinch of chili powder
salt and freshly ground black pepper
olive oil, for sautéing
a little all-purpose flour, for dusting

FOR GARNISH
coriander leaves
lemon wedges

1 Drain the chick-peas and rinse under cold running water. Put them in a large saucepan and cover with fresh cold water. Bring to a boil, then lower the heat and simmer for at least 1 hour, until very tender, adding more boiling water to the pan if necessary. Drain thoroughly.
2 Pass the chick-peas through a vegetable mill or grinder, then transfer to a bowl and mash with a fork to make a smooth, thick purée. Or work the chick-peas in a blender or food processor until puréed.
3 Stir in the onion together with the parsley, garlic, coriander, cumin and chili. Season to taste with salt and pepper. Cover and refrigerate for at least 1 hour.
4 Preheat the oven to 225°F.
5 Scoop up tablespoons of the mixture and, with floured hands, shape into flat cakes 1 inch across.
6 Heat 2 tablespoons olive oil in a large skillet, add one-third of the falafel and sauté gently [!] for about 5 minutes, turning once very carefully with a fish turner, until brown and crisp. Drain well on absorbent kitchen paper and transfer to a warmed serving dish. Keep warm in the oven while frying the remainder in 2 batches, adding more olive oil as needed. Drain on absorbent kitchen paper, arrange with the other falafel on the serving dish and garnish with coriander leaves and lemon wedges. Serve at once (see Serving ideas).

Cook's Notes

TIME
Cooking the chick-peas takes about 1 hour; making the purée takes about 2-3 minutes in a food processor, about 10 minutes by hand. Allow 1 hour chilling time. Shaping and cooking the falafel take about 25 minutes.

FREEZING
Cool the fried, drained falafel completely, then flash freeze until solid. Transfer to a rigid container, seal, label and freeze for up to 2 months. To serve: Sauté from frozen.

BUYING GUIDE
To save time, buy two cans (16 oz size) chick-peas. Drain and rinse, then continue the recipe from the beginning of stage 2.

SERVING IDEAS
Serve the falafel with a tangy lemon-flavored mayonnaise. For a filling lunch, serve the falafel inside a pocket of pita bread with a salad of sliced tomatoes, cucumber and watercress, and coleslaw and plain yogurt.

WATCHPOINT
Turn the falafel very carefully in the skillet, so that they do not break. To make cooking easier, first dip in beaten egg, then in flour.

●70 calories per falafel

LEBANON

Every Lebanese restaurant serves chicken cooked with garlic and lemon – it may be pieces of chicken or a squab, marinated and broiled or cooked in the oven, or kabobs of boned chicken. Broiling, especially over charcoal, is a favorite way of cooking in the Lebanon. In this version, *Jaaj meshwi*, the chicken pieces are coated in spices before broiling, and are served with a cold purée of eggplants, olive oil, lemon juice and garlic.

Lebanese broiled chicken

SERVES 4
1 (3-3½ lb) broiler-fryer, cut in 8 pieces (see Buying guide)
juice of 4 large lemons
¼ cup olive oil
2 large cloves garlic, crushed
½ teaspoon salt
pinch of ground allspice
pinch of ground cinnamon
freshly ground black pepper

FOR GARNISH
parsley or coriander sprigs
lemon and tomato wedges

1 Place chicken pieces in a large dish.
2 Put the lemon juice, oil, garlic and salt in a blender and work for a few seconds (see Cook's tip).
3 Sprinkle the allspice, cinnamon and pepper over the chicken and rub into the skin.
4 Pour the lemon juice mixture over the chicken and rub in thoroughly. Cover and let marinate in a cool place for at least 8 hours or overnight, turning the pieces from time to time.
5 Preheat the broiler to medium and brush the broiler rack with oil.
6 Broil the chicken pieces for about 20-30 minutes, brushing frequently with the marinade, until cooked through (the juices should run clear when the thickest part is pierced with a skewer) and the skin is crisp.
7 Transfer the cooked chicken to a warmed serving dish, garnish with parsley or coriander and lemon wedges and tomato. Serve at once with the eggplant purée (see recipe and Serving ideas).

Eggplant purée

SERVES 4
1 lb eggplants
3 tablespoons olive oil
about 2 tablespoons lemon juice
1 clove garlic, crushed
salt and freshly ground black pepper

1 Preheat the broiler to high. Arrange the eggplants in the broiler pan and heat under the broiler until the skins start to blister and the eggplants are soft to the touch.
2 Put the eggplants in a colander and rinse under cold running water, then peel off the skins (see Illustration, right).
3 Squeeze the eggplants over a bowl to remove the bitter juices, then chop the flesh roughly and place in the goblet of a blender (see Cook's tip). Add oil, 2 tablespoons lemon juice and garlic and season to taste with salt and pepper. Work to a smooth purée.
5 Taste the purée and add more lemon juice if liked. Transfer to a serving dish and refrigerate until the purée is required.

SKINNING EGGPLANTS

1 *Arrange the eggplants on the rack and heat until skins blister and the eggplants are soft.*

2 *Rinse under cold running water, then peel the eggplant skins off in thick strips with a sharp knife.*

Cook's Notes

Lebanese broiled chicken

TIME
Preparation takes about 15 minutes and cooking 20-30 minutes. Allow at least 8 hours for marinating the chicken before cooking.

BUYING GUIDE
If preferred, buy 4 large chicken pieces, and cut each piece in half.

COOK'S TIP
Blending the marinade emulsifies the mixture, making a creamy sauce which does not separate while the chicken is marinating.

WATCHPOINT
When broiling chicken on the bone it is very important to cook it right through to bone. If necessary, cook for longer, on lower heat.

SERVING IDEAS
Serve on a bed of bulgur wheat and parsley salad, with a tomato, pepper, carrot and zucchini mixed salad.

●500 calories per portion

Eggplant purée
TIME
Total preparation takes about 20 minutes.

DID YOU KNOW
This is a version of poor man's caviar – so called because it tastes a little like real caviar, yet costs far less.

COOK'S TIP
If you do not have a blender, put eggplant in a bowl and mash with a fork.

●105 calories per portion

EGYPT

Ful medames (pronounced fool maydamez) can be truly regarded as Egypt's national dish. It is eaten by everyone, from the richest to the poorest, and is found on menus in smart restaurants and sold by street vendors. The basic dish is simply cooked beans, but it can be seasoned and flavored in many different ways – one Cairo restaurant offers 15 varieties of *Ful medames*.

Ful medames

SERVES 4-6

2½ cups dried Egyptian brown beans, soaked overnight (see Buying guide)
4½ teaspoons ground cumin
4 large cloves garlic, crushed
¼ cup olive oil
5 cups water
1 teaspoon mild paprika
1 teaspoon ground turmeric
salt and freshly ground black pepper

TO SERVE
about ⅔ cup olive oil
3 lemons, cut in wedges
coriander leaves
5 tablespoons chopped fresh parsley
6 hard-cooked eggs (see Variations)

1 Drain the soaked beans and rinse thoroughly. Put them into a large saucepan and add the cumin, garlic, olive oil and water.
2 Bring to a boil, boil for 5 minutes then lower the heat, cover and simmer for 1-1½ hours, or until beans are tender and there is just enough juice left in the pan to coat the beans. The water evaporates during the long cooking, leaving a small amount of thick, spicy, gravy-like juice.
3 Transfer the beans and juice to a large serving bowl, sprinkle over paprika and turmeric and season the mixture with plenty of salt and pepper. Stir well.
4 To serve: Put a small pitcher of olive oil on a tray or large serving platter. Garnish the lemon with coriander and add this to the tray together with the parsley and hard-cooked eggs.
5 Serve the beans hot or warm and pass the tray of accompaniments separately.

Cook's Notes

TIME

Preparing, cooking and finishing this dish take 1½-2 hours. Allow for overnight soaking of the beans.

BUYING GUIDE
Egyptian brown beans may be sold as Ful medames beans. They are small, round and brown and are sold at many specialist Middle Eastern delicatessens.

SERVING IDEAS
It is traditional for each person to crumble a hard-cooked egg over his beans with a squeeze of lemon juice and olive oil and chopped parsley added to taste.

The beans can also be served with the following selection: Feta cheese, scallions, watermelon or sweet melon slices, olives, pickled cucumber, a garlic-flavored tomato sauce and hot pita bread. Arrange them on a large tray so that everyone can help himself.

VARIATIONS
The hard-cooked eggs can be replaced by the traditional *hamine* eggs or Jewish *Hamindas*, which are baked brown eggs (see Illustrations).

Add some of the following to the dried beans while they are cooking; sliced green or sweet red peppers, tomatoes, chili sauce and red lentils, for color as well as flavor.

The water used for cooking the beans may be replaced with vegetable stock but use the unsalted variety – salt toughens the beans.

Canned Egyptian brown beans are sold in many specialist stores and delicatessens. They do not need to be soaked and cooked so are ideal for this recipe if you are in a hurry: simply drain off most of the juice from four cans (16 oz size), then stir in 4 cloves garlic, crushed, 3 tablespoons olive oil, 4½ teaspoons ground cumin. Season with salt and pepper.

●895 calories per portion

PREPARING HAMINE EGGS

1 Bring eggs to a boil in water with 1 teaspoon oil and ½ teaspoon salt. Gently transfer eggs to an ovenproof dish.

2 Add the cooking water and ½ an unpeeled, sliced onion. Cover and bake in a preheated 225°F oven for 8-12 hours until dark brown.

NORTH AFRICA

Couscous grain is a type of hard-wheat semolina. In Morocco and other North African countries, it is steamed over a rich broth, to make a favorite national dish. The word *couscous* comes from the sound the steam makes as it pushes through the holes of the steamer.

Couscous is ideal for serving a large number of guests as it is best prepared in large quantities, preferably a day in advance. The broth may include any fresh or dry vegetable and any type of meat or fish, flavored with spices.

Couscous

SERVES 10

2 lb stew lamb, cut in large
    pieces (see Buying guide)
2 chicken quarters, cut in large
    pieces (total weight 1½ lb)
1 lb stew beef or veal, cut in large
    pieces (see Buying guide)
⅓ cup chick-peas, soaked in cold
    water for at least 1 hour
2 large onions, minced
2 cloves garlic, chopped (optional)
½ teaspoon ground ginger
1 teaspoon ground cinnamon
3 whole cloves
freshly ground black pepper
⅓ cup seedless raisins or golden
    raisins
6 dried dates, pitted and chopped
2 small turnips, quartered
2 carrots, sliced
½ small white cabbage, shredded
salt
4 zucchini, sliced
⅔ cup hulled fresh or frozen
    fava beans
2 tomatoes, peeled and chopped
6 tablespoons chopped fresh parsley
6 tablespoons chopped fresh
    coriander (optional, see Did you
    know)
3 lb medium or fine-ground
    pre-cooked couscous (see
    Buying guide)
⅓ cup vegetable oil or ¼ cup
    butter
1 teaspoon mild paprika
generous pinch of cayenne or
    chili pepper

Cook's Notes

TIME
Preparation takes about 1½ hours, including soaking the chick-peas. Cooking takes about 2 hours.

BUYING GUIDE
Ask your butcher for any cheap cut of lamb, such as neck. Chuck or flank are good beef stewing cuts, and the veal often sold in butchers as "stew veal" would be suitable.

Pre-cooked couscous (steamed, processed and dried) is available in packages from Middle Eastern food stores or specialist delicatessens.

WATCHPOINT
Do not add any salt until the chick-peas begin to soften, or they will go tough.

DID YOU KNOW
Fresh coriander leaves as well as seeds are widely used in Middle Eastern cooking, and can sometimes be obtained from Middle Eastern and Oriental food shops.

In the Middle East, the dish is prepared in a special *couscousier*, a cooking pot with a steamer section on top, not unlike a double boiler.

PREPARATION
The usual method for preparing pre-cooked couscous is to place it with a pinch of salt in a bowl, cover with boiling water and leave to soak for about 15 minutes, stirring occasionally, until the liquid is absorbed.

COOK'S TIPS
The soaked couscous may just be heated through in a saucepan, but steaming gives a grainier result.

● 980 calories per portion

1 Put the lamb, chicken and beef in a very large saucepan (see Did you know). Cover with fresh cold water, bring to a boil and remove the foam with a skimmer or slotted spoon.
2 Drain the chick-peas and add to the pan with the onions, garlic, if using, ginger, cinnamon, cloves and pepper to taste. [!] Cover the pan and simmer for 1 hour.
3 Add the raisins, dates, turnips, carrots, cabbage and salt to taste, and simmer for a further 30 minutes.
4 Add the zucchini, fava beans, tomatoes, parsley and coriander, if using, and simmer for a further 30 minutes.
5 Prepare the pre-cooked couscous according to package directions (see Preparation), then mix in the vegetable oil. Place the couscous in a large colander and set it over the vigorously boiling broth in the saucepan (see Cook's tips). When steam begins to rise through the strainer or colander, the couscous is done.
6 To make the sauce: Measure out a large cupful of broth, strain and then stir in the mild paprika and cayenne.
7 To serve: Pile the couscous in a pyramid on a warmed round serving platter. Remove the meats and vegetables from the broth with a slotted spoon and arrange them on top of the couscous. Serve the broth in a warmed bowl with a ladle. Pass the hot sauce separately in a pitcher, so your guests can help themselves.

KENYA

The tropical island of Lamu lies just above the equator, very close to the northern coast of Kenya in East Africa. Spices grow in abundance there and are widely used to enhance the local food. The islanders live almost exclusively on rice, fish and coconuts, all of which are combined in this very popular dish, called *Samaki wa Lamu* in Swahili.

Lamu-style fish

SERVES 4-6

2 lb haddock fillets, thawed
   if frozen, skinned and cut in
   2 × 1 inch pieces (see
   Did you know)
4 cloves garlic, crushed
juice of 2 limes
1½ teaspoons ground cumin
1 teaspoon salt
1 teaspoon freshly ground black
   pepper
3 tablespoons sunflower oil
lime slices, for garnish

1 In a small bowl, mix the garlic and lime juice to a paste with the cumin, salt and pepper. Spread the mixture over the fish. Set aside on a plate while cooking the rice (see recipe).

2 When rice is cooked heat oil in a large skillet, add fish and sauté over moderate heat for 8 minutes, turning carefully with a fish turner halfway through. Drain on absorbent kitchen paper.
3 Arrange the fish on a warmed serving dish, garnish with lime slices and serve at once.

Coconut rice

SERVES 4-6

1¼ cups long-grain rice,
   washed and drained
1 cup cubed creamed coconut
   (see Buying guide)
   or 2 cups shredded coconut
1¼ cups hot water
3 tablespoons sunflower oil
1 tablespoon salt

1 Put the creamed coconut pieces into a bowl, pour over the hot water and stir until the coconut has dissolved. If using shredded coconut, pour over 4 cups boiling water (the coconut will retain some water), leave to infuse for 20 minutes. Strain, pressing coconut with back of spoon to extract as much liquid as possible.
2 Heat the oil in a heavy-bottomed saucepan, add the drained rice and stir until each grain is coated with oil. Pour in the coconut liquid to just cover, topping up with a little boiling water if necessary. Add the salt, stir well and bring to a boil. Cover the pan, turn down the heat as low as possible and simmer for 12-15 minutes or until the rice is tender and all the liquid has been completely absorbed.
3 Remove the coconut rice from the heat and keep in a warm place until ready to serve.

Cook's Notes

Lamu-style fish

TIME
Preparation 10 minutes, cooking about 8 minutes.

DID YOU KNOW
In Lamu, the firm-fleshed kingfish would most likely be used. (Do not confuse this with the American kingfish, which is an oily fish, not unlike mackerel). Haddock makes an excellent substitute.

SERVING IDEAS
Lightly cooked spinach mixed with sautéed onion and tomato and flavored with mild curry powder makes a delicious accompaniment to the fried fish and coconut rice. In Lamu, the fish, rice and accompanying vegetables would be served on separate brass platters. You may, however, prefer to arrange the fish on a large serving dish with the rice in a ring around it.

For a festive touch, serve the accompaniments in hollowed-out coconut shells.

This dish is served for the evening meal locally. It would be followed by sticky, fudge-like candies and Turkish-style coffee flavored with cardamom or ginger. Because Lamu has been visited by Arab spice traders since the Middle Ages, the island's culture, reflected in its food, is a fascinating blend of Arab and African characteristics.

●255 calories per portion

Coconut rice

TIME
Preparation takes about 5 minutes, cooking about 12-15 minutes.

BUYING CODE
Creamed coconut is the shredded flesh of the coconut, drained of liquid and pressed into a solid block. It is widely used in Asian cooking and is available from Asian food stores and large supermarkets.

DID YOU KNOW
A cone made of plaited grass – a *kawa* (see photograph) – is used to cover food before serving.

●510 calories per portion

CANADA

Each spring in the maple woods of Canada the sap begins to rise in the trees, and the clear fluid is transformed in sugaring cabins to rich, amber-colored maple syrup. Canada also produces very fine ham and in this recipe for Maple ham the two make a delicious, uniquely Canadian combination. Serve the baked, clove-flavored ham with traditional cornbread muffins, made with cornmeal, which Canadians call Johnny cakes.

Maple ham

SERVES 6-8

1 (5 lb) boneless shank half ham
15-20 cloves

FOR GLAZE
½ cup maple syrup
3 tablespoons light brown sugar
1 teaspoon dry mustard

1 Cover the ham with cold water and let soak for 3-4 hours.
2 Preheat the oven to 375°F.
3 Dry the ham with absorbent kitchen paper. Using a sharp knife and kitchen shears, if necessary, remove the skin and some of the fat below it. Using a sharp knife, score the fat surface of the ham in a trellis pattern, cutting about ¼ inch deep. Stud the intersections with cloves (see Illustration).
4 Weigh the ham and calculate the cooking time at 35 minutes per 1 lb. Put the ham in a roasting pan and bake in the oven for the calculated cooking time.
5 Meanwhile, make the glaze: Combine the maple syrup, sugar and dry mustard in a bowl and stir well to mix.
6 Forty-five minutes before the end of the calculated cooking time, remove the ham from the oven and spoon half the glaze over the scored surface. Return to the oven for 15 minutes, then spoon over the remaining glaze and bake for the remaining 30 minutes, until golden brown. Transfer to a warmed serving platter and serve hot.

HOW TO TRELLIS HAM

1 *Score the fat surface in a trellis pattern with a sharp knife.*

2 *Stud the centers of the trellis with cloves.*

Raisin sour cream pie is a typical example of the Canadian way of mixing together unusual ingredients. With a rich sweet dough that tastes equally good hot or cold, this pie can be served as an alternative to mince pies at Christmas or pumpkin pie on Thanksgiving Day.

Raisin sour cream pie

MAKES 6-8 SLICES
2½ cups all-purpose flour
2 teaspoons baking powder
pinch of salt
⅓ cup superfine sugar
¼ teaspoon vanilla
1 egg, separated
1 tablespoon milk
⅔ cup diced butter or margarine
milk, for brushing

FILLING
1¼ cups seedless raisins
⅔ cup sour cream
1 teaspoon ground cinnamon
¼ teaspoon ground cloves
¼ teaspoon freshly grated nutmeg
2 eggs
⅓ cup brown sugar
½ cup pecan nuts, chopped (see Buying guide)

1 Preheat the oven to 400°F.
2 Make the filling: Put the raisins into a large bowl and stir in the sour cream and spices. Mix well, then set aside while making dough.
3 Sift the flour, baking powder and salt into a bowl. Make a well in the center and add the sugar, vanilla, half the egg yolk and all the egg white and the milk. Stir until well mixed together.
4 Beat the butter into the mixture, then knead lightly to form a smooth dough. Wrap in plastic wrap and refrigerate for 30 minutes.
5 Roll out half the dough on a lightly floured surface and use to line a 9 inch pie pan.
6 Beat the eggs in a small bowl, then stir into the sour cream and fruit mixture. Stir in the brown sugar and nuts and mix well.
7 Pour the filling into the pie shell and smooth top with a knife.

Cook's Notes

TIME
Preparation, including chilling the dough, takes 1 hour. Cooking takes 30 minutes, plus 15 minutes cooling.

SERVING IDEAS
Serve the raisin pie warm with a pitcher of heavy cream for a special dessert, or leave until cold, slice and serve with coffee.

BUYING GUIDE
Pecan nuts are available ready-packaged in most supermarkets. They are most often used in Pecan pie (see page 86) but are delicious in the combination used here. Pecans are related to walnuts, which may be used instead, though walnuts have a more pronounced flavor. Golden raisins may be used but the color combination will not be so striking.

FREEZING
Leave pie until cold, then wrap in a plastic bag, seal, label and freeze for up to 2 months. To serve: Thaw for 3-4 hours, then cover the pie in foil and warm in a preheated 350°F oven for about 20-25 minutes.

●655 calories per slice

Roll out remaining dough and use to make a crust. Prick top with a fork, then mix the remaining egg yolk with a little milk and brush the top crust.
8 Bake the oven for 30 minutes or until the pastry is golden brown. Remove from the oven and let cool for 15 minutes. Remove from pan ✳ and serve warm or cold.

UNITED STATES

Maryland is well known for the fine quality of the chickens raised there, and has given its name to a fried chicken dish now famous the world over. There are many variations of the true Chicken Maryland, some of which have been passed down from mother to daughter in hand-written family cookbooks. But the real thing is always served with a cream gravy and "corn oysters" – delicate corn fritters.

This version of the recipe comes from an old Baltimore family; its "two-coat" method of creating a deliciously crispy crust is said to have been devised by a family cook long before the Civil War.

The "Chicken Maryland" with fried bananas and bacon that is so popular in many other countries is very tasty in its own way but it bears little resemblance to the genuine article.

Chicken Maryland

SERVES 6

6 chicken pieces (total weight about 3½ lb), thoroughly thawed if frozen

3 cups milk (see Variations)
2 cups all-purpose flour (see Variations)
2½ teaspoons salt
pinch of cayenne
freshly ground black pepper
¾ cup shortening
1 tablespoon all-purpose flour, for gravy

1 Wash the chicken and pat dry with absorbent kitchen paper. Arrange in a single layer in a large roasting pan and pour over 1¼ cups of the milk. Cover with plastic wrap and refrigerate for about 30 minutes.
2 Remove the chicken pieces, and set the roasting pan of milk aside. Put the 2 cups flour in a plastic bag with the salt, cayenne and pepper to taste. Shake well to mix, then add the chicken pieces one or two at a time. Shake the bag vigorously until the chicken is well coated in the seasoned flour.
3 When all the pieces have been floured, dip them in the reserved milk in the roasting pan, then toss them again in the bag of seasoned flour.
4 Preheat oven to 225°F.
5 In a large, heavy skillet, melt enough shortening to come to a depth of about 1½ inches. Heat until very hot, then lower the heat and cook the chicken pieces, ⚠ skin side down, until brown on one side, then turn them carefully and cook until brown on the other side.

Cook's Notes

TIME
Preparation takes 40 minutes, including chilling the chicken parts. Cooking the chicken takes just under 1 hour, and making the gravy about 8 minutes.

VARIATIONS
For an even richer dish, use 2½ cups milk and make up to 3 cups with light cream.

All-purpose white flour is traditional for this recipe, but wholewheat flour gives a nuttier coating.

WATCHPOINT
The chicken must be fried slowly and turned frequently so that the crust is not broken.

SERVING IDEAS
Mashed potatoes or rice go very well with Chicken Maryland, since they absorb the cream gravy well.

● 355 calories per portion

Continue to cook over low-to-moderate heat, turning the pieces frequently, for about 30 minutes or until the chicken is thoroughly cooked (the juices should run clear when the thickest part is pierced with a fine skewer).
6 Remove the chicken pieces, drain quickly on absorbent kitchen paper, then arrange on a warmed serving platter. Keep hot in the oven while making the gravy and corn oysters.
7 Make the cream gravy: Pour the fat from the skillet into a heatproof bowl. Measure out 2 tablespoons, and pour this amount back into the skillet. Stir in 1 tablespoon flour and cook, stirring, for about 1 minute, then gradually stir in the remaining 1¾ cups milk.
8 Bring slowly to a boil, stirring constantly, then lower the heat and simmer until the gravy is thick, scraping up the sediment from the base and side of the pan. Pour the gravy into a warmed gravy boat and keep hot in the oven with the chicken while cooking the corn oysters.

Corn oysters

SERVES 6
¾ cup all-purpose flour
½ teaspoon baking powder
generous pinch of salt
1 can (10 oz) creamed corn
2 eggs
bacon drippings or shortening

1 Sift the flour, baking powder and salt together onto a plate. Put the corn in a bowl.
2 Beat the eggs until light and fluffy. Add them to the corn and mix well. Fold in the flour mixture until no trace of flour is visible in the batter.
3 Generously grease a heavy skillet or griddle with bacon drippings, and heat until a drop of water flicked over the surface splutters. Cook the corn oysters in batches, dropping heaped teaspoonfuls of the corn mixture into the pan, about 1 inch apart. Cook over high heat until the "oysters" are brown underneath. Turn them with a spatula or fish turner and cook on the other side until brown.
4 When the "oysters" are ready transfer them to a baking sheet lined with absorbent kitchen paper and keep warm in the oven with the chicken until all the chicken pieces are cooked. Serve as soon as they are all ready, arranged around the fried chicken on a serving platter or on a separate dish.

Cook's Notes

TIME
Preparing the corn mixture takes 3-4 minutes, and cooking the corn oysters about 15 minutes.

DID YOU KNOW
Corn oysters are so called because they are oyster-shaped and taste rather like batter-fried oysters, which are another specialty of Maryland and other coastal regions of the United States.

● 130 calories per portion

Gumbo – an African work for okra – became the name of a hearty soup traditional to Louisiana when okra was brought to the American Deep South by the African slave ships in the 18th century. Okra, a tapering green vegetable which is actually the seed pod of a type of hibiscus, is a main ingredient of this delicious soup, which is poured over freshly cooked rice to serve. Gumbo may be made with a variety of seafood, but this shirmp version is the most popular, since shrimp is so plentiful along the Louisiana coast.

Shrimp gumbo

SERVES 4
1 lb okra, thinly sliced (see Buying guide)
1 lb shelled shrimp, thawed if frozen
¼ cup butter
1 onion, finely chopped
1 green pepper, seeded and finely chopped
1 clove garlic, crushed
2 tablespoons all-purpose flour
4 cups chicken stock
½ lb tomatoes, peeled and chopped
bouquet garni (2 sprigs parsley, 1 sprig thyme, 1 bay leaf)
good pinch of cayenne
salt and freshly ground black pepper

1 Melt the butter in a large saucepan, add the onion, green pepper and garlic and sauté gently for 5 minutes until the onion is soft and lightly colored. Sprinkle in the flour and cook for a further 2 minutes, stirring constantly with a wooden spoon.
2 Pour in the chicken stock, stir well and bring to a boil. Add the okra, tomatoes, bouquet garni and cayenne, and season to taste with salt and pepper. Lower the heat, cover the pan and simmer very gently for 20 minutes, until the okra is very tender.
3 Remove and discard the bouquet garni. Add the shrimp and cook gently for a further 2-3 minutes, stirring once or twice, until they are heated through.
4 Serve the gumbo in warmed deep soup bowls over Lemon rice (see recipe on next page).

Lemon rice

SERVES 4

1¼ cups long-grain rice
2 tablespoons butter
1 tablespoon lemon juice
½ teaspoon salt and a little freshly
  ground black pepper
1½ cups water

1 Rinse the rice several times under cold running water, then drain.
2 Put the rice, butter, lemon juice, salt and pepper in a large saucepan. Pour in the water. Bring quickly to a boil. Stir once, then cover and cook over very gentle heat for about 20 minutes until all the liquid is absorbed and the rice is tender.
3 Leave the rice to stand, covered, for about 10 minutes, then spoon a portion into each of 4 soup bowls and pour over the shrimp gumbo.

Texas produces some of the world's finest beef, so it is not surprising that spicy Chili con carne (*con carne* means "with meat") is enormously popular there. This Texan chili is adapted from the Mexican version, which originally used beef introduced to the New World by Spain.

Chili con carne traditionally consists of cubed or ground beef and dried red chilies (hot chili powder gives excellent results in place of dried chilies). In Mexico it is sometimes thickened with *masa harina*, the corn-meal used to make Mexican *tortillas* or pancakes. Onions, tomatoes and garlic may also be included in the chili; cooked red kidney beans can be added just before the end of cooking time, or served separately.

Easy to prepare and very tasty, Chili con carne (see Did you know) is perfect for a family meal or informal party; just adjust the quantities according to the number you have to feed.

Chili con carne

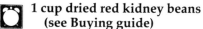

SERVES 4
1 cup dried red kidney beans
   (see Buying guide)
3 onions, finely chopped
1 bay leaf
3 tablespoons vegetable oil
1 lb lean beef, ground
   (see Buying guide)
1 clove garlic, crushed
2 teaspoons dried oregano
1 teaspoon ground cumin
1 teaspoon chili powder
1 tablespoon mild paprika
freshly ground black pepper
1 can (16 oz) tomatoes, roughly
   chopped, with their juice
1¼ cups beef stock
salt

1 Wash and pick over the beans, then place in a large bowl and cover with cold water. Let soak for 8 hours, preferably overnight.
2 Drain the soaked beans, rinse thoroughly under cold running water, then put them into a large saucepan with one-third of the chopped onions and the bay leaf.

Pour in fresh cold water to cover and bring to a boil. Boil fast for 10 minutes. ⚠ Reduce the heat to low, cover the pan, and leave the beans to simmer for 1½-2 hours. During cooking check the pan from time to time and add extra boiling water as needed.

3 Start to cook the meat when the beans have been cooking for about 30 minutes. Heat the oil in a large, heavy skillet. Add the beef, the remaining onions and the garlic, and cook until the beef is lightly browned, breaking it with a wooden spoon.

4 Transfer the beef mixture to a 4 quart Dutch oven. Add the oregano, cumin, chili powder, mild paprika and black pepper to taste. Stir well to mix. Add the tomatoes with their juice and the beef stock. Simmer, partially covered for 1-1½ hours until the beef is tender.

5 About 15 minutes before the meat is ready, test the beans; by now they should be almost tender. Add 2 teaspoons salt to the pan. Continue to boil until the beans are tender, without adding more water. ⚠ Strain and drain thoroughly.

6 Add the beans to the meat mixture in the pot, stir gently but thoroughly and continue to simmer for 10-15 minutes, until heated through. Serve the Chili con carne at once straight from the pot.

Cook's Notes

 TIME
Preparation and cooking take about 2½ hours. Remember to soak the beans for 8 hours or overnight.

 VARIATIONS
Fresh tomatoes, peeled, can be used instead of canned.

If you like a slightly hotter chili, add more chili powder to taste.

SERVING IDEAS
Serve with boiled rice and a green salad. Baked jacket potatoes also go well with this dish. Cold beer or lager, or iced lime juice would be refreshing to drink with this hot dish.

 FREEZING
Cool quickly, then pack in a plastic bag or rigid container. Seal, label and freeze for up to 2 months. To serve: Thaw from frozen in a heavy-bottomed saucepan until bubbling, stirring constantly and adding a little water if the mixture seems dry.

BUYING GUIDE
Take care to buy pulses from a store with a quick turnover; stale pulses will never become tender however long they are soaked and cooked. Even pre-packaged pulses need to be washed, to remove any dirt or grit remaining.

Instead of buying ground beef from the supermarket or butcher, buy good-quality chuck or round steak and grind it yourself – the result will taste infinitely better; the ready-prepared ground beef can be very fatty.

 COOK'S TIP
Chili con carne can be made the day before and refrigerated overnight. Let it come to room temperature for about 2 hours before reheating until bubbling.

⚠ WATCHPOINTS
It is essential to boil red kidney beans for 10 minutes before simmering them, to destroy a poisonous enzyme present in the beans.

Do not add any more water after salting the beans, as the cooked beans should be quite dry. If necessary, finish off the cooking with the pan uncovered, to make any surplus liquid evaporate more quickly.

? DID YOU KNOW
Chili is a Spanish and Mexican word meaning hot red peppers. Although the full title of the dish is *chili con carne*, it is usually only referred to as *chili*.

The long cooking time is intentional because of the chili powder in the recipe. If only cooked for a short time, the finished dish will taste raw and the flavor of the chili will not have time to mature and be absorbed into the meat.

●520 calories per portion

Pecan pie originated in the American Deep South, where the early settlers in the seventeenth century found pecan nut trees growing in Georgia. Nowadays there are almost as many "classic" pecan pie recipes as there are American states. One famous Georgian cook of the 1920s, Mrs James Sutcliffe, insisted on including molasses to make her pie filling even richer.

Because of the richness of the filling, most people prefer pecan pie made with basic pie dough, as in our recipe. But some New Orleans cooks make it with *pâte brisée* (pie dough enriched with egg yolk), reflecting their French heritage. Some recipes use an unbaked pie shell, so that the filling seeps right through the crust during cooking. Our version, from Georgia, is made with a pie shell baked blind, to give the base a slightly crunchy texture.

Pecan pie

SERVES 8

½ lb basic pie dough,
    thawed if frozen

FILLING
1 cup light brown sugar
¾ cup light corn syrup
6 tablespoons butter (see Cook's tip)
½ teaspoon salt
3 large eggs
1¼ cups pecan halves (see Buying guide)
1 teaspoon vanilla

1 Preheat the oven to 450°F.
2 Roll out the dough thinly on a lightly floured surface and use it to line a 9 inch pie plate. Reserve the trimmings. Brush the edges of the dough with a little water.
3 Roll out trimmings to an 8 × 2 inch rectangle. Cut in 3 strips. Twist strips at regular intervals (see Illustration) and brush one side with a little water. Press the moistened sides around edge of plate (see Illustration) and press to seal joints.
4 Prick the pie shell in several places with a fork. Place a circle of waxed paper or foil in the pie shell; weight it down with a thick, even layer of baking beans. Bake blind for 8-10 minutes.
5 Meanwhile, put the sugar, syrup, butter and salt in a small heavy-bottomed saucepan and heat gently until the sugar is completely dissolved. Remove from the heat.
6 Remove the pie shell from the oven, remove the foil and beans and let the pie shell cool. Lower oven heat to 350°F.
7 Beat the eggs well in a bowl, then

TIME
Preparing the pie shell, baking blind and making the filling takes about 40 minutes. Baking in the oven takes about 50 minutes. Allow 30 minutes cooling time, then 1 hour chilling.

SERVING IDEAS
Always serve pecan pie cold, cut in small wedges as it is very rich and filling. Unsweetened whipped cream makes a very good accompaniment.
Pecan pie makes an excellent addition to a picnic; pack it in the pie plate in which it was baked.

WATCHPOINT
If the edge browns too fast as the pie bakes, cover it with a strip of foil to prevent it burning.

COOK'S TIP
Butter is an essential ingredient in the pie filling. Do not be tempted to use margarine instead as this will be a false economy; the pie will not have the right flavor.

STORAGE
Pecan pie keeps well. Covered with plastic wrap, it can be stored in the refrigerator for up to 1 week.

BUYING GUIDE
Pecan nuts are similar in appearance to walnuts, to which they are related, but are longer with a more oval shape, and have a sweeter taste. They should be a glossy deep brown and firm and slightly brittle, not limp or dull-looking. They are available ready-packaged in health food stores and some delicatessens. Walnuts may be used instead.
It is worth buying more pecan nuts than you need for this recipe – they will be cheaper this way. Store those you do not use in an airtight container and use them to make cookies.

● 500 calories per slice

MAKING THE TRIMMING

1 *Twisting the dough strips for the edge of the pie.*

2 *Press the twisted dough strips around the edge of the pie plate.*

---

gradually stir in the melted syrup mixture. Reserve eight of the best pecan halves. Coarsely chop the remainder and stir into the filling mixture. Stir in the vanilla and beat well.
8 Pour the filling mixture evenly into the prepared pie shell and carefully arrange the reserved pecan halves in a circle around the edge.
9 Bake the pie in the oven for 40-50 minutes, ⟨!⟩ until the center of the filling is beginning to set. Cool, cover the pie with plastic wrap and refrigerate for at least 1 hour. Serve cold (see Serving ideas).

MEXICO

Avocados were cultivated in Mexico as far back as 7000 B.C. and *guacamole,* made from mashed avocados with spicy flavorings, is an ancient Mexican dish which remains as popular today as it has ever been. It can be served in a variety of ways, but is most often eaten as a dip.

Guacamole

SERVES 4
2 ripe avocados (see Buying guide)
¼ lb peeled tomatoes,
   seeded and finely chopped
1 tablespoon minced onion
   (see Cook's tips)
1 teaspoon hot green chili pepper,
   seeded and finely chopped (see
   Variations)
1 tablespoon finely chopped fresh
   coriander leaves or flat-leaved
   parsley
salt
lemon slice and parsley, for garnish

1 Cut the avocados in half and remove the seeds. Scoop out the avacado flesh with a spoon and put it in a large bowl. Mash the avocado flesh well with a fork until it is smooth and creamy.
2 Add all the other ingredients and mix very thoroughly to blend (see Cook's tips).
3 Transfer the guacamole mixture to a serving bowl. Fork it up and garnish with a lemon twist and parsley sprigs. Serve the guacamole at once (see Cook's tips).

Cook's Notes

TIME
Preparation takes only 10 minutes.

COOK'S TIPS
Do not exceed this amount of chopped onion or the flavor of the avocado will be lost.

Although the ingredients are finely chopped, the guacamole should have a slightly chunky texture, with a definite "bite" to it. So, combine the ingredients by hand, not in a food processor, or the mixture will be too smooth.

As avocado discolors easily, guacamole should be served as soon as it is ready. Otherwise, cover the bowl with plastic wrap and chill in the refrigerator until required; just before serving, turn the surface over with a fork if it has discolored slightly.

There is a theory that placing the avocado seed in a dish containing an avocado mixture prevents it from discoloring. Although many people swear by it, there is no actual scientific proof that it works!

BUYING GUIDE
To test for ripeness, press the thin end of the avocado gently; it is ripe if the flesh "gives" slightly. To avoid bruised avocados, buy them when underripe and leave them on a sunny windowsill for a few days to ripen slowly.

DID YOU KNOW
Guacamole gets its name from *aguacate*, the Mexican word for avocado.

VARIATIONS
A dash of hot pepper sauce may replace the chopped chili pepper.

SERVING IDEAS
In Mexico, guacamole is usually served with fried wedges of *tortilla*, a type of pancake in which a special flour called *masa harina*, made from boiled maize, is used.

Potato chips or sliced pita bread would be excellent for scooping up the guacamole, or it can be served with a selection of crudités as an appetizer with drinks.

Try guacamole as an opener or side salad, served in individual bowls lined with lettuce leaves. Alternatively, scoop out raw large tomatoes and fill them with guacamole to make an unusual vegetable accompaniment.

Guacamole also makes a delicious sauce with poached or baked white fish or cold meat such as chicken, turkey or pork.

●165 calories per portion

BRAZIL

This rich chocolate mousse, with its deliciously different flavor, is very popular with the Brazilians who love sweet dishes, and it combines two ingredients native to South America; chocolate and cashew nuts. Chocolate, which originated in Mexico, was drunk by the ancient Aztecs before it was discovered by the Spaniards in the 16th century, while cashew nuts, which grow profusely and are used extensively in Brazil, are even included in the making of an alcoholic drink called *cajuada*.

Mousse de castanhas de caju e chocolate

SERVES 6-8

2 squares (2 oz) dark unsweetened chocolate, broken in small pieces (see Buying guide)
3 tablespoons hot water
½ cup superfine sugar
5 eggs, separated
1 cup cashew nuts, finely ground (see Buying guide and Preparation)
1¼ cups heavy cream
pinch of salt
few whole cashew nuts, to decorate

1 Put the chocolate in the top of a double boiler or a bowl set over a saucepan of simmering water. Add the water and sugar and stir with a wooden spoon over low heat until the chocolate is completely melted and the sugar fully dissolved (see Illustration).
2 Off heat, remove the top section of the double boiler or the bowl from the hot water. Using a balloon whip, beat in the egg yolks one at a time, beating well after each addition until they are fully incorporated. Set the chocolate and egg mixture aside to cool for about 15 minutes.
3 Lightly stir the ground cashew nuts into the cooked chocolate and egg mixture.
4 Put 1 cup of the cream and the egg whites in separate clean dry bowls. Whip the cream until standing in soft peaks. Beat the egg whites until standing in stiff peaks. Using a large metal spoon, lightly fold first the cream, then the beaten egg whites into the chocolate and ground cashew nut mixture.
5 Pour the mixture into a glass serving bowl, cover with plastic wrap and refrigerate overnight or until the mousse is set.
6 Just before serving, whip the remaining cream until standing in soft peaks. Pipe rosettes of cream around the edge of the mousse and top each rosette with a cashew nut. Serve the chocolate and cashew nut mousse chilled with cookies, if liked (see Serving Ideas).

Cook's Notes

TIME
Preparation takes about 25 minutes, then allow for overnight chilling. Finishing the chocolate mousse takes about 5 minutes.

COOK'S TIP
This is a perfect dessert to serve at a dinner party; as it it needs to be made the day before to ensure that it sets and that the flavors develop, there is only the decoration to do on the night of the party.

PREPARATION
Grind the nuts in a blender, food processor or coffee grinder. They must be finely ground, but avoid over-grinding, or they will be reduced to a paste.

●495 calories per portion

BUYING GUIDE
Unsweetened chocolate is ideal for this recipe. Semisweet chocolate or chocolate chips may be used but, in this case, cut down slightly on the sugar.
Cashew nuts are roasted before they are edible, as the nut shell contains a toxic oil which must be removed by the roasting process. Shelled cashews are available plain or salted; use plain nuts for this recipe.

SERVING IDEAS
Serve the mousse with crisp *langues de chat* cookies or ladyfingers, if liked.
Follow the rich mousse with small cups of strong, piping hot black coffee and a glass of Tia Maria liqueur for a special occasion; the coffee flavor complements chocolate perfectly.

TWO WAYS TO MELT CHOCOLATE

1 *Melt the broken-up chocolate in a flameproof bowl set over a pan of simmering water.*

2 *Melt the chocolate in the top of a double boiler.*

USSR

This sumptuously rich dish was the brainchild of a 19th century French chef, who was faced with the hazards of a Siberian winter and the demands of his gourmet Russian patron, Count Stroganoff. Frustrated in his attempts to cope with permanently frozen beef, the chef decided to cut it in tiny, thin strips, then sauté it and serve it in a sour cream and mushroom sauce. The result seems to have found favor with the Count.

Beef Stroganoff

SERVES 4

[!] **1 lb fillet steak, trimmed of fat (see Buying guide)**
freshly ground black pepper
2 tablespoons vegetable oil
¼ cup butter
1 onion, thinly sliced
2 cups thinly sliced small button mushrooms
1¼ cups sour cream (see Buying guide)
2-3 teaspoons Dijon mustard, according to taste
salt
chopped fresh parsley, for garnish

1 Lay the meat flat and beat it well with a wooden rolling pin. Cut it in ¼ inch thick slices. Cut each slice across the grain in ¼ inch wide strips, 1-2 inches long (see Illustration). Sprinkle with pepper and set aside.

2 Heat half the oil and butter in a wide shallow pan, add the onion and saúte over low heat for 10 minutes until soft and golden, stirring frequently.

3 Increase the heat a little, add the mushrooms and sauté for a further 2 minutes, stirring constantly. Cover the pan, remove from the heat and set aside.

4 Heat the remaining oil and butter in a separate, large shallow skillet. When sizzling hot, add half the beef strips and sauté over high heat [!] for about 1 minute, turning constantly until the beef is sealed.

5 Remove the meat from the pan with a slotted spoon and keep hot in the covered pan with the onion and mushrooms. Sauté the remaining meat in the same way.

6 Stir the sour cream and mustard into the beef and vegetables, add salt and pepper to taste, then place over gentle heat and bring to just below the boiling point, stirring constantly.

7 Spoon the Beef Stroganoff onto warmed individual dishes. Garnish the top of each portion with a sprinkling of chopped fresh parsley and serve the Stroganoff at once, piping hot (see Serving ideas).

Cook's Notes

 TIME
Allow about 20 minutes for preparing the meat and vegetables and another 20 minutes for cooking.

 BUYING GUIDE
All parts of a fillet of beef are very tender; the pointed rib end is usually less expensive than the thick center cuts, and is perfectly suitable for this dish.
   If sour cream is unavailable, simply stir 2 teaspoons lemon juice into 1¼ cups fresh heavy cream.

●445 calories per portion

 VARIATIONS
Thinly sliced tenderloin of pork, or veal or lamb kidneys, can be used to make a delicious pork or kidney Stroganoff.

 SERVING IDEAS
Because it is a rich dish, only a plain accompaniment is needed; spoon onto a bed of boiled rice or noodles. Serve a green salad separately.

[!] **WATCHPOINT**
The strips of beef must be sautéed rapidly to seal in the juices and keep the meat succulent.

PREPARING STRIPS OF BEEF

1 With a sharp knife, cut the fillet steak lengthwise in slices ¼ inch thick.

2 Cut each slice across the grain of the meat in ¼ inch wide strips, 1-2 inches long.

Chicken Kiev was created in and named after the beautiful capital city of the Ukraine, in the south-west of the USSR. In this internationally renowned dish, the chicken breasts are stuffed with garlic butter, then deep-fried until the crumb coating is golden and crisp, and the meat inside tender and succulent.

Chicken Kiev

SERVES 4

4 chicken breast and wing pieces, skinned, each weighing about ½ lb (see Buying guide)
½ cup butter, softened
¼ teaspoon finely grated lemon rind
2 teaspoons lemon juice
1-2 cloves garlic, finely crushed
1 tablespoon finely chopped fresh parsley
salt and freshly ground black pepper
2 tablespoons all-purpose flour
1 cup fine dry white bread crumbs
2 eggs
vegetable oil, for deep frying
French rib frills, to finish
parsley sprigs and lemon wedges, for garnish

1 Put the butter, lemon rind and juice, garlic and parsley in a small bowl, with salt and pepper to taste. Beat with a wooden spoon until smoothly blended.

2 Transfer to a flat plate and shape into a rectangle 2½ inches long. Cover butter and refrigerate for at least 4 hours until firm. ⚠

3 Prepare the chicken breasts: With a sharp knife, remove any breastbone and cut away the wing tips just below the first joint.

4 Lay the chicken breasts on a board or working surface, skinned side down and with the thickest part toward you. Make a pocket in each breast by slitting the breast horizontally, taking care not to pierce the flesh at either end or on the far side (see Illustration).

5 Cut the block of butter lengthwise in 4 equal fingers. Insert into the pockets and then close the pockets

(see Illustration).

6 Spread the flour and bread crumbs out on separate flat plates and season the flour well with salt and pepper. Beat the eggs in a shallow dish.

7 Dip each stuffed chicken breast first in flour, to coat thoroughly all over, tapping off the excess. Then dip in beaten egg and finally in bread crumbs, to coat thoroughly. Press the coating on firmly with a spatula. Dip the coated breasts again in egg, then in bread crumbs. Press the coating on again, transfer to a plate, cover and refrigerate for 1-2 hours, to firm the coating.

8 Preheat the oven to 225°F.

9 Pour enough oil into a deep-fat fryer to come halfway up the sides. Heat to 350°F or until a stale bread cube browns in 60 seconds. ⚠ Lower 2 of the chicken breasts into the hot oil and fry for 12-15 minutes, turning once, until golden and cooked through.

10 Remove the cooked chicken breasts from the oil, drain on absorbent kitchen paper and keep hot in the oven while frying the remaining chicken breasts in the same way.

11 Slip a French rib frill onto each wing joint. Arrange the chicken breasts on a warmed serving dish, garnish with parsley sprigs and lemon wedges and serve at once. ⚠

Cook's Notes

TIME
Allow 4 hours chilling time for the butter. Preparing the chicken breasts takes about 30 minutes, then allow a further 1-2 hours chilling time. Frying takes about 30 minutes.

BUYING GUIDE
Large, thick, firm chicken breasts are required for Chicken Kiev. The wing joint is essential so that the dish may be finished professionally with a French rib frill. Order the breast and wing pieces in advance from the butcher.

SERVING IDEAS
Serve Chicken Kiev with crisp, golden straw potatoes and peas in pastry boats or round tarts. Alternatively, serve the chicken with creamed spinach flavored with freshly ground nutmeg, and croquette potatoes.

●535 calories per portion

VARIATIONS
Strongly flavored garlic butter is an integral part of Chicken Kiev; the quantity of garlic may be varied. However, if you do not care for garlic, try a variation of the dish; use 1 tablespoon finely snipped chives instead. Alternatively the butter may be flavored with 1 tablespoon finely chopped fresh parsley and a seasoning of onion salt to taste.

WATCHPOINTS
Chilling the garlic butter for at least 4 hours is essential; it must be ice cold and quite firm so that it melts slowly as the chicken is frying.

The frying temperature is critical; if the oil is too hot, the coating will overbrown before the chicken is cooked.

Be sure to provide table napkins when serving Chicken Kiev; the liquid butter tends to spurt out when the chicken breast is cut.

MAKING A "POCKET" IN THE CHICKEN

1 *Make a slit horizontally to within 1 inch of each end.*

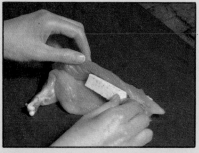

2 *Insert a finger of chilled garlic butter lengthwise into pocket.*

3 *Press the edges of pocket firmly together to enclose butter.*

Pashka means Easter in Russian, and is the name given to the sweet, creamy dessert with dried fruits and almonds traditionally served in Russia at Easter. *Pashka* is eaten after the Russian Orthodox midnight Easter service in which the congregation celebrates the Resurrection of Christ, amidst glorious singing and a blaze of candles.

The *pashka* dessert was originally made in a pyramid-shaped wooden mold carved with the Russian letters XB (standing for *Christos voskrese,* "Christ is risen" in Russian), the Russian Orthodox cross and the Easter symbols of an egg, and a cockerel. It was eaten with *kulich,* a sweet yeast bread which was served surrounded by brightly colored Easter eggs.

Pashka is very rich, containing eggs, cream and butter, ingredients forbidden by the Russian Church during Lent. In flavor and texture *pashka* is rather like cheesecake. Tea, served Russian-style in glasses, without milk and with a slice of lemon if liked, goes well with it.

Pashka

SERVES 6-8

3 cups small-curd cottage cheese
½ cup sweet butter, softened
3 eggs, separated
½ cup superfine sugar
3 tablespoons heavy cream
½ vanilla bean
½ cup chopped blanched almonds
½ cup seedless raisins

TO DECORATE
cut mixed candied peel
candied cherries and angelica
whole blanched almonds

1 Cut out a large piece of scalded cheesecloth to line a new 6 inch diameter flowerpot (see Illustration).
2 Using a wooden spoon, beat the small curd cottage cheese and butter together in a bowl until very smooth. Set aside.
3 Put the egg yolks and sugar in a separate bowl. Beat with a balloon whip until thick and creamy.
4 Put the cream and vanilla bean in a small, heavy-bottomed saucepan and bring slowly to just below the boiling point. Remove the vanilla bean.
5 Allow the cream to cool very slightly, then pour slowly onto the egg mixture, beating constantly.
6 With a large metal spoon, fold the egg and cream mixture into the cheese and butter mixture. Fold in the almonds and raisins, so that they are evenly distributed.
7 Beat egg whites until standing in stiff peaks and fold into mixture.
8 Carefully pour the mixture into the prepared flowerpot (see Illustration). Fold the cloth over, place a plate on top and weight down.
9 Put the flowerpot on a wire rack in a shallow dish so as much liquid as possible drains from *pashka* while setting. Refrigerate 24 hours.
10 Remove the weight and plate. To unmold, invert a round serving plate on top of the flowerpot, then gently invert, holding pot and plate firmly. Carefully remove the flowerpot and peel away the cheesecloth.
11 Decorate the top and sides of the *pashka* with peel, cherries, angelica and almonds. Press gently but firmly into surface, so they adhere.

PREPARING AND FILLING THE FLOWERPOT

1 *Line the flowerpot with scalded cheesecloth, pressing the cloth well into the edge around the bottom and leaving plenty of material around the edge to fold over the top.*

2 *Pour the pashka mixture into the lined flowerpot, then fold the edges of the cloth neatly over the top of the pot. Place a small plate inside the pot and weight down.*

Cook's Notes

TIME
Preparation takes about 20 minutes. Allow 24 hours draining and setting. Finishing takes 15 minutes.

SERVING IDEAS
The *pashka* may be served as a dessert at the end of a meal, or for tea. The Italian yeast cake with dried fruits called *panettone,* available from Italian delicatessens and specialist food stores, is very like the Russian *kulich* with which *pashka* was traditionally served, and would make a good accompaniment. Or, serve the *pashka* with a light sponge cake.

DID YOU KNOW
The original Russian *pashka* contains considerably more sugar, and the egg whites are not beaten. It also needs 36 hours draining.

●600 calories per portion

CHINA

One of the delights of eating out Chinese style is the range of appetizing dishes on offer. Some of these, however, are deceptively simple to make and can quite easily be prepared at home.

Give your dining table a real flavor of the Orient by serving a dish of sweet and sour pork, accompanied by fried rice and stir-fried broccoli.

For Chinese fried rice, boil the rice for 15 minutes until not quite tender, drain and spread out to cool. Heat some vegetable oil in a large skillet and sauté the rice, stirring constantly with a wooden spoon, for 3-5 minutes. Diced meat, shrimp and sliced vegetables stir-fried in the same way, make tasty and colorfully attractive additions to the rice.

For the table decoration, go Chinese and float single flower heads such as a chrysanthemum, dahlia or marguerite in small bowls of water. White flowers in white bowls look particularly elegant. And for a finishing touch, bring out the chopsticks!

Chinese sweet and sour pork

SERVES 4

! 1½ lb pork tenderloin
1 tablespoon cornstarch
salt
vegetable oil, for deep-frying

SAUCE
1 teaspoon cornstarch
¼ cup water
2 tablespoons wine or cider vinegar
2 tablespoons brown sugar
2 tablespoons orange juice
1 tablespoon tomato paste
2 tablespoons soy sauce
pinch of cayenne
1 small onion, minced
1 tablespoon vegetable oil
½ green pepper, seeded and cut in thin strips
½ red pepper, seeded and cut in thin strips

MAKING SCALLION TASSELS

1 *Trim the scallions of most of the green tops and remove the thin skin and the bulb end. With a small sharp knife, make several slits close together from top to bulb end of scallion.*

2 *Place the scallion in a bowl of ice water for 1 hour. The tops will curl back to make an attractive "tassel". Drain thoroughly and use to garnish the edge of the serving platter.*

1 To make the sauce: Put the cornstarch into a bowl and then gradually pour on the water, stirring all the time to form a smooth mixture. Stir in the vinegar, sugar, orange juice, tomato paste, soy sauce, cayenne and half the minced onion.

2 Trim away any excess fat from the pork and cut in 1 inch cubes. Season the cornstarch with a pinch of salt and put it into a brown paper or plastic bag. Toss the meat cubes in it, a few at a time, to coat them thoroughly. Remove the meat and shake off any excess cornstarch.

3 Heat the oil in a deep fryer to a temperature of 375°F on a cooking thermometer, or until a small cube of bread turns golden brown in 50 seconds. Fry half the meat for about 6-8 minutes, until it is crisp and golden brown. Remove with a slotted spoon, drain it on crumpled absorbent kitchen paper and keep it warm while you fry the remainder of the meat.

4 Heat the tablespoon of vegetable oil in a skillet, add the remaining chopped onion and strips of green and red pepper. Sauté over high heat for 1 minute, lower the heat to moderate, then pour in the sauce. Stir for a few minutes until the sauce is bubbling and thickened. Add the

cooked cubes of pork and stir carefully. Cook for 1 minute only, to blend the flavors. Turn the Chinese sweet and sour pork and sauce into a warmed serving dish and serve at once.

Cook's Notes

TIME
Preparation and cooking take 35 minutes.

VARIATION
Cubes of lamb or chicken can be cooked and stirred into the sauce in the same way. Small cubes of chicken will deep-fry in 5-6 minutes.

! WATCHPOINT
Cook the meat in batches in a deep fryer or wok – do not try to cook it all together in a small pan of oil because the meat will lower the temperature of the oil too much, and it will not cook to the characteristic crispness that is important in this dish.

●680 calories per portion

Stir-fried broccoli

SERVES 4

1½ packages (10 oz size) frozen
   broccoli, thawed
2 scallions
2 tablespoons vegetable oil
½ teaspoon salt
1 tablespoon soy sauce
2 tablespoons dry sherry

1 Drain the broccoli. Cut in 2 inch
strips and cut the stems in half
lengthwise if thick.
2 Slice the scallions, discarding
most of the green ends.
3 Heat the oil in a large skillet. Add
the onions and salt and sauté over
high heat for 30 seconds. Add the
broccoli, lower the heat to moderate
and stir for 3 minutes.
4 Pour on the soy sauce and sherry.
Continue to stir for 2 minutes until
the vegetables and sauce are very
hot. Serve at once.

Cook's Notes

TIME
Cooking time is 10
minutes, but allow 1
hour for the broccoli to thaw.

COOK'S TIP
Use fresh broccoli if
available. Cook it in
boiling salted water for 3
minutes then drain thoroughly
before stir-frying.

● 85 calories per portion

An essential principle of the ancient Chinese philosophy known as Taoism is that harmony arises from the proper blending of opposites (the *yin-yang* principle). This belief is also reflected in Chinese cooking, of which a main feature is the balance of colors, flavors and textures. This Cantonese recipe illustrates this harmony perfectly.

Cook's Notes

 TIME
Preparation takes about 25 minutes, marinating 30 minutes and the cooking less than 5 minutes.

COOK'S TIPS
Beat the steak between 2 sheets of waxed paper to tenderize as well as flatten it to the required thickness before cutting into strips.

1 tablespoon light soy sauce and 1 tablespoon dark soy sauce may be used, if liked, for a darker color.

If the snow peas are small, leave them whole – if they are large, it is better to cut them in half.

A wok with a long wooden handle is best for stir-frying (a two-handled wok is suitable for steaming).

! WATCHPOINTS
When stir-frying both the snow peas and the beef, add the stock only if absolutely necessary; the dish should not be served in a thin, runny sauce.

Do not keep the snow peas in the oven – they will lose their bright green color.

 VARIATION
If snow peas are not available, use a large green pepper, seeded and finely shredded.

● 190 calories per portion

Beef with snow peas

SERVES 4

¾ lb round steak, cut across grain in 1½ × 1 × ¼ inch strips (see Cook's tips)
1 tablespoon cornstarch
1 tablespoon dry sherry
2 tablespoons light soy sauce (see Cook's tips)
1 teaspoon salt
1½ teaspoons sugar
¼ cup vegetable oil
½ lb snow peas, cleaned (see Cook's tips and Variation)
1 tablespoon chicken stock (optional)
2 scallions, finely chopped
2 slices fresh gingerroot, finely chopped

1 In a large bowl, blend the cornstarch with the sherry and soy sauce to a smooth paste. Add a pinch of the salt and 1 teaspoon of the sugar. Stir in the beef strips, then cover and leave to marinate for about 30 minutes stirring once. Meanwhile boil 12 oz rice to accompany the dish. Cool before stir-frying.

2 Heat a long-handled wok for 1½ minutes (see Cook's tips). Heat half the oil in the wok. When it is smoking, add the snow peas, stir over brisk heat until evenly coated with oil, then add the remaining salt and sugar and stir-fry for 1-1½ minutes, adding a little chicken stock if the peas show signs of sticking. [!] Transfer the snow peas to a warmed serving dish, cover and keep in a warm place while cooking the beef.[!]

3 Wash and dry the wok, heat it again, then add the remaining oil. Heat until smoking, then add the scallions and gingerroot and stir.

4 Using a slotted spoon, lift the beef strips from the marinade, draining off any excess, and add to the wok. Stir over brisk heat until evenly coated with oil, then stir-fry for 1 minute, adding a little chicken stock if the beef shows any signs of sticking. Spoon the beef over the snow peas and serve at once, accompanied by fried rice, passed separately in a warmed serving bowl.

A popular and wonderfully tasty stir-fried mixture of meat and vegetables, *Chop suey* did not actually originate in China itself. It is believed to have been invented by pioneering Chinese restaurateurs in the United States at the height of the nineteenth-century Gold Rush.

Chop suey

SERVES 4
½ lb pork tenderloin, trimmed of excess fat
2 teaspoons cornstarch
1 tablespoon dry sherry
2 tablespoons soy sauce
2 scallions
2 slices fresh gingerroot
½ head cauliflower
2 carrots
1 small green pepper
2 cups fresh beansprouts (see Cook's tips)
3 tomatoes
⅓ cup vegetable oil
1 teaspoon salt
1 teaspoon sugar
a little chicken stock (optional)

1 Cut the pork lengthwise in four 1½ inch slices, then cut each into slices about ¼ inch thick. Place in a shallow dish.
2 In a small bowl, blend together the cornstarch, sherry and soy sauce to make a smooth paste. Pour the mixture over the pork, stir well to mix, then cover and let marinate while you prepare the vegetables.
3 Cut the scallions in ½ inch strips. Peel and finely chop the gingerroot. Break the cauliflower into flowerets, discarding the leaves and any thick fibrous stems. Thinly slice the carrots. Seed and finely shred the green pepper. Trim the beansprouts of any husks. Slice the tomatoes.
4 Heat 3 tablespoons oil in a wok (see Cook's tips) or large skillet until it is just smoking. Add the sliced pork and stir with a long-handled spoon or spatula for 2-3 minutes until each slice is coated with oil. Transfer the pork slices to a plate with a slotted spoon.
5 Heat the remaining oil in the wok and add the scallions and slices of

CLEANING A WOK

After use, wash under hot water; do not use detergent. Brush or scour with soapless scourer, then dry thoroughly over moderate heat to prevent rusting.

Always season a new wok before use: Wash in hot water, dry over moderate heat and wipe inside with a pad of absorbent kitchen paper soaked in vegetable oil.

fresh gingerroot to delicately flavor the oil.
6 Add the cauliflower flowerets and sliced carrots to the wok or skillet and cook, stirring all the time, for 1 minute.
7 Add the green pepper, beansprouts and tomatoes and cook, stirring all the time for 1 further minute. Season with salt and sugar and stir a few more times until heated through.
8 Add the pork slices, moisten with a little stock if necessary (see Cook's tips) and stir for 30 seconds. Taste and adjust seasoning, transfer to a warmed dish and serve at once (see Serving ideas).

JAPAN

The idea of deep-frying food was introduced to Japan by the Portuguese in the 16th century, and *tempura* – pieces of fish, shellfish, meat and vegetables coated in a light batter, deep-fried and served with a tasty sauce – is now one of Japan's favorite dishes. Tempura is a perfect example of the Japanese taste for cooking food quickly, in order to help preserve the naturally fresh, delicate flavor of the ingredients.

In Japan's climate the four seasons are very distinct, and each of them has its own characteristic foods. The Japanese like to include at least one seasonal ingredient in *tempura*. They might include bamboo shoots for spring; okra or asparagus for summer; chrysanthemum or maple leaves for autumn and sweet potato for winter.

Tempura

SERVES 4

12 jumbo shrimp, body shell removed and tails left on (see Illustration)
4 mushrooms, stems removed
1 large carrot, cut in matchsticks
1 large green pepper, seeded and cut in 8 pieces
1 onion, cut in ¼ inch slices
2½ cups sunflower oil, for deep frying (see Cook's tips)

SAUCE

⅔ cup Japanese soup stock (see Buying guide) or water
2 tablespoons soy sauce
pinch of salt
2 teaspoons sugar
1 cup finely shredded white radish (see Buying guide)

BATTER

1 cup all-purpose flour, sifted
1 egg, lightly beaten
¾ cup cold water

1 Make the sauce: Stir together all the ingredients except the radish in a small saucepan. Bring to a boil, remove from heat and set aside.
2 Make the batter: In a bowl quickly mix together all the ingredients (see Cook's tips) until blended.
3 Heat the oil in a deep-fat fryer to 350°F or until a bread cube browns in 60 seconds.
4 Quickly dip the ingredients in the batter and fry in batches, starting with the vegetables (see Cook's tips), until puffed and golden.
5 Transfer to individual plates (see Did you know).
6 Stir the radish into the sauce in the pan, pour into 4 individual small bowls and serve at once with the tempura (see Cook's tips).

Cook's Notes

TIME
Preparation takes about 30 minutes and frying about 10 minutes.

COOK'S TIPS
Sunflower oil gives the best flavor to tempura; corn oil is also suitable.

Mixing the batter quickly ensures that the tempura has a light, crisp thin batter coating through which the colors of the food can be seen. Over-stirring makes the batter heavy and gives a "bready" result. In Japan the batter is mixed with bamboo cooking chopsticks.

Cook the vegetables first, to ensure that they do not have a fishy taste. Fry only enough ingredients at once to cover half the surface of the oil; if too many are fried the temperature of the oil is lowered and the food will not cook properly.

Tempura is best eaten as soon as it is fried, so be sure to have everything ready to serve when it is cooked.

BUYING GUIDE
Japanese food stores sell instant soup stock (called *dashinomoto*), made from kelp and flaked dried bonito fish. Dissolve 1 tablespoon in ⅔ cup hot water for a very tasty sauce.

There are a number of varieties of radish apart from the familiar red-skinned salad radishes. White radish is a long tapering root which probably originated in southern Asia; in Japan a variety called *daikon* radish is widely used in cooking – shredded as a garnish and in sauces, sliced in vegetable mixtures and pickled to eat with various kinds of fish.

White radish is sold in oriental food stores. There is a similar vegetable called mooli. If you cannot obtain either, use grated horseradish.

DID YOU KNOW
In Japan, plates or racks of meshed bamboo are often used for serving tempura, lined with special absorbent tempura paper which is sold ready-cut to size in packages.

It is usual in Japan to serve food on individual plates, not from a serving platter; this is an extension of a past tradition when the diners used to sit at separate tables.

A Japanese meal normally consists of 4 or 5 dishes which are served at the same time and eaten in no particular order. The selection might consist of a main dish such as tempura or raw fish, pickled vegetables, rice and soup. Saké (Japanese rice wine), beer or white wine would be served with the meal.

●250 calories per portion

REMOVING THE BODY SHELL FROM A JUMBO SHRIMP

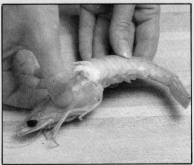

1 *Straighten the shrimp as much as possible and then pull off the head with a twisting movement.*

2 *Insert fingers under the legs and pull up over the saddle to remove shell and leave tail intact.*

INDONESIA

Saté, the Malay word for spiced sauce, is also the name of one of the most popular of all dishes eaten in Indonesia. A saté consists of marinated cubes of meat threaded onto skewers, broiled and served with a spicy peanut sauce on a bed of rice.

Chicken saté with peanut sauce

SERVES 4

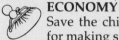

4 large chicken leg pieces, each weighing about ¾ lb
1 small onion, minced
1 small green pepper, seeded and very finely chopped
3 tablespoons soy sauce
2 tablespoons lemon juice
1 tablespoon vegetable oil
1 teaspoon dark brown sugar

PEANUT SAUCE
½ cup shredded coconut
1 cup boiling water
5 tablespoons crunchy peanut butter
2 teaspoons dark brown sugar
½ teaspoon chili powder

1 Cut the chicken in bite-size pieces, discarding skin and bones (see Illustration below, and Economy). Put the chicken in a bowl.

2 Mix the minced onion with the green pepper, soy sauce, lemon juice, oil and brown sugar. Pour the mixture over the chicken, stir well, then leave to marinate in a cool place for at least 2 hours, turning the meat occasionally.

3 Meanwhile, prepare the sauce: Put the coconut into a bowl and pour over the boiling water. Cover with a saucer or plate and let stand for 15 minutes. Strain into a small saucepan, pressing all the liquid out of the coconut with the backs of your fingers. Discard the coconut. Add the remaining sauce ingredients to the pan, mix well and set aside.

4 Preheat the broiler to moderate.

5 Drain the chicken, reserving the marinade. Thread the chicken onto 4 oiled long skewers, leaving a slight gap between each piece. Remove the rack from the broiler pan, place the skewers in the pan and pour over 2-3 tablespoons marinade.

6 Broil for about 15 minutes, turning and basting occasionally with more marinade until cooked

through. Remove from the broiler and keep hot.

7 Add all the marinade and the juices from the broiler pan to the peanut sauce. Bring to a boil, stirring, then lower heat and simmer for 1-2 minutes.

8 To serve: Put the saté on a bed of yellow rice and pass the sauce separately. Serve at once.

BONING THE CHICKEN

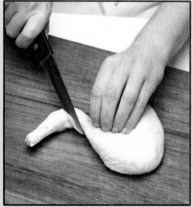

1 Put the chicken piece on a board. Using a sharp knife, cut off the bottom scaly leg joint, if necessary.

2 Pull away skin and fat, then turn fleshy side down. Slit leg flesh through to bone. Ease leg flesh away from bone.

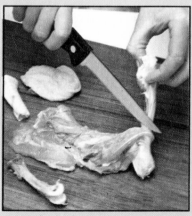

3 Break the 2 leg joints and pull out the leg bones. Ease remaining meat from bones and discard them or use for stock.

Yellow rice

SERVES 4

1¾ cups long-grain rice
2 tablespoons vegetable oil
1 teaspoon ground turmeric
2 cups chicken stock
¼ teaspoon ground cinnamon
1 bay leaf

1 Heat the oil in a saucepan, add the rice and stir over moderate heat for 2 minutes. Add the turmeric, lower the heat and cook, stirring, for a further 1-2 minutes.

2 Pour in the stock, ⚠ add the cinnamon and bay leaf and stir well.

3 Bring to a boil, then lower the heat and cover with a tight-fitting lid. Cook over the lowest possible heat for 15 minutes or until all the liquid has been absorbed and the rice is tender. ⚠ Remove the bay leaf and serve hot.

Cook's Notes

TIME
20 minutes to simmer and cook the rice.

SERVING IDEAS
Serve a cool cucumber relish with the saté: Mix together a pared, thinly sliced cucumber with 2 sliced scallions, juice of 1 lemon, sugar and pepper to taste.

WATCHPOINTS
Stand well back when you add the stock to the pan of sautéed rice; the mixture will splutter and spit.

The rice must cook over the lowest heat, or the liquid evaporates too fast and the rice becomes dry before it is cooked.

●395 calories per portion

The Indonesians are especially fond of dishes made from lightly cooked, crisp and crunchy vegetables. Peanuts feature prominently in Indonesian cooking, and *Gado-gado* – which means "a mixture" – is topped with a nutty savory sauce. It is one of the most popular dishes throughout the Indonesian islands.

Gado-gado

SERVES 4
1 potato, scrubbed but unpeeled
1½ cups shredded green cabbage or collard greens
⅔ cup sliced green beans
⅔ cup thinly sliced carrots
½ head cauliflower, divided in flowerets
1 bunch of watercress, divided in sprigs
2 cups beansprouts

SAUCE
1 cup shelled raw peanuts (see Buying guide)
vegetable oil, for cooking
1 clove garlic, crushed
2 shallots or ½ small onion, minced
salt
½ teaspoon chili powder
½ teaspoon light brown sugar
1½ cups water
juice of 1 lemon

FOR GARNISH
1 large egg, hard-cooked and cut in wedges
1 head lettuce, shredded
¼ cucumber, sliced
1 onion, sliced in rings and sautéed until crisp and brown
prawn crackers, fried (see Buying guide)

1 Make the sauce: Heat enough oil in a large, heavy skillet or wok to cover the peanuts. Add the peanuts and sauté over moderate heat for 5-6 minutes, stirring occasionally. Remove the peanuts with a slotted spoon and drain on absorbent kitchen paper. Let cool. Pour all but 1 teaspoon of the oil out of the pan.
2 Grind the cooled peanuts to a fine powder in a food processor or coffee grinder, or pound them, using a pestle and mortar.
3 Reheat the oil in the pan, add the garlic and shallots, season with salt and fry for 1 minute. Stir in the chili powder and sugar and add the water. Bring the mixture to a boil, then stir in the ground peanuts. Lower the heat and simmer, stirring occasionally, for 4-6 minutes until the sauce thickens. Set aside.
4 Bring 3 saucepans of salted water to a boil. Add the potato to one pan and boil gently for 15 minutes.
5 Meanwhile, add the cabbage, green beans, carrots and cauliflower to another pan and boil gently for 4 minutes.
6 Add the watercress and bean-sprouts to the third pan and boil gently for 2-3 minutes.
7 Drain all the vegetables very thoroughly. Let the potato cool slightly, then cut in thin slices.
8 Pile the cabbage, green beans, carrots, cauliflower, watercress and beansprouts onto a round serving dish (see Cook's tip). Arrange the potato slices and hard-cooked egg wedges on top, and arrange the shredded lettuce and sliced cucumber around the edge.
9 Stir the lemon juice into the sauce in the pan and heat through gently. Pour the sauce over the salad. Garnish with sautéed onion rings and prawn crackers, broken in small pieces. Serve at once.

Cook's Notes

TIME
Preparing the vegetables takes 20-30 minutes. Making the sauce and cooking the vegetables take about 45 minutes. Assembling the salad and reheating the sauce take about 10 minutes.

BUYING GUIDE
Buy raw peanuts; roasted or salted peanuts will not give the right flavor or texture.
Prawn crackers made from rice flour and prawns, are available in packages from Chinese food stores, oriental delicatessens and some large supermarkets; sauté them according to package directions. Or use shrimp-flavored potato chips instead for the garnish.

SERVING IDEAS
Gado-gado makes a delicious appetizer or side salad to accompany a fairly light main-course dish. Try it with fish, chicken or stir-fried pork.
With extra potato and egg added, Gado-gado makes an excellent snack lunch.

DID YOU KNOW
If you are serving Gado-gado with fish, and would like to give the sauce a seafood flavor, try adding a shrimp paste called *terasi*, available from Chinese food stores. It is very highly flavored and needs to be used sparingly; crush a piece about the size of a hazelnut and cook it with the shallots and garlic.
You can make an "instant" sauce for Gado-gado using *satay* powder from Chinese food stores.

COOK'S TIP
The salad is best served with the vegetables still just warm.

●335 calories per portion

Madras beef curry, which is as hot and colorful as the region of Madras itself, was developed by the Moslems and Christians of southern India (Hindus, to whom the cow is sacred, never eat beef). Lime pickle is the traditional accompaniment – its tartness cleverly offsetting the rich spiciness of the beef.

Madras beef curry

SERVES 4

1½ lb best-quality bottom round
  steak, cut in 1 inch cubes
  (see Buying guide)
4 tablespoons ghee
1 onion, thinly sliced
2 cloves garlic, minced
2 teaspoons coriander seeds
2 teaspoons ground turmeric
1 teaspoon chili powder
1 teaspoon ground coriander
1 teaspoon ground cumin
1 teaspoon freshly ground black
  pepper
3 inch piece fresh gingerroot,
  finely chopped
2½ cups boiling water
4 green chilies, cut in ¼ inch
  pieces (see Cook's tips and
  Watchpoint)
1 teaspoon salt
2 teaspoons garam masala
coriander leaves and lime slices,
  for garnish

1 Melt the ghee in a large, heavy bottomed saucepan, add the beef cubes and sauté over moderate heat, turning, to seal and brown on all sides. Remove the beef cubes with a slotted spoon, transfer them to a plate and set aside while preparing the spicy sauce.

2 Add the onion to the pan and cook gently for 5 minutes until soft and lightly colored. Add the garlic, coriander seeds, turmeric, chili powder, ground coriander and cumin, pepper and ginger. Add ¼ cup of the boiling water and stir well.

3 Add the beef cubes to the pan and stir well to coat with the spice mixture. Pour in the remaining water, add the chopped chilies and stir well again. Cover the saucepan and simmer for 45-60 minutes, until the beef is tender when pierced with a sharp knife (see Cook's tips). Add the salt and garam masala and stir well to mix.

4 Transfer the beef to a warmed serving dish, garnish with coriander leaves and lime slices and serve at once (see Serving ideas).

Hot lime pickle

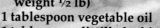

thinly pared rind and
  juice of 3-4 limes (total
  weight ½ lb)
1 tablespoon vegetable oil
1 tablespoon distilled white
  vinegar
1 tablespoon chili powder
1 teaspoon ground turmeric
2 green chilies, finely chopped

1 Put all the ingredients except the lime rind into a blender or food processor. Work for a few seconds until the mixture is smooth and thoroughly blended.

2 Cut the lime rind into matchstick strips and put them into a 2 lb screw-top jar. Pour over the sauce, cover tightly with the lid and shake the jar well. Leave the hot lime pickle in a cool place overnight to allow the flavors to develop before serving with the curry (see Storage).

Cook's Notes

Beef curry

TIME
Preparation, including the precooking, takes about 25 minutes. Cooking then takes 45-60 minutes.

SERVING IDEAS
Serve with plain boiled fluffy white rice, fried or broiled poppadoms and hot lime pickle (see recipe). Cold beer is the ideal drink to accompany this spicy, hot Madras beef curry.

! WATCHPOINT
Wash your hands as soon as you have finished chopping the chilies; the juice can sting the eyes quite badly should you happen to rub them.

COOK'S TIPS
Most heat from chilies is in the seeds. For a milder curry remove the seeds from chilies during preparation, then rinse chilies.

According to the age and therefore the dryness of the spices, different amounts of water will be absorbed. Add a little more boiling water if the dish shows signs of becoming dry. The sauce should be fairly thick; if necessary, once the beef is cooked, increase the heat and cook, uncovered, until the liquid is reduced.

BUYING GUIDE
Chuck or flank are both suitable for this recipe.

●470 calories per portion

Hot Lime pickle

TIME
Preparation takes about 15 minutes. Allow overnight infusing time.

COOK'S TIP
Pickles made from limes, mangoes or chilies are extremely popular with Indians. The sharpness of these fruits helps counteract the hot taste of the curry.

STORAGE
Although the pickle can be served within 1 day of making, the flavor will improve with storing. The pickle will keep for up to 3 months in the refrigerator.

●35 calories per portion

The *korma* is widely regarded as a superior example of Indian cuisine, far from any run-of-the-mill curry dish. Containing a number of luxurious ingredients – saffron, poppy seeds, cashew nuts and cream – *kormas* are mostly reserved for feast days and holidays.

Chicken korma

SERVES 4

1 (3-3½ lb) broiler-fryer,
   divided in 8 pieces and skin
   removed (see Illustration)
1 lemon, halved
1 tablespoon salt
1¼ cups plain yogurt
½ teaspoon saffron threads
1 tablespoon poppy seeds
2 inch cinnamon stick, broken
   in small pieces
1 teaspoon chili powder
1 teaspoon dried coriander seeds
1 teaspoon ground cumin
½ teaspoon freshly ground black
   pepper
2 tablespoons water
¼ cup ghee or vegetable oil
   (see Buying guide, page 115)
1 onion, thinly sliced
1 clove garlic, crushed
2 inch piece fresh gingerroot,
   cut in thin strips
10 cardamom pods
10 cloves
½ cup unsalted cashew nuts
⅔ cup heavy cream
coriander leaves, for garnish

1 Rub the chicken with the lemon. Squeeze the juice over a bowl large enough to hold chicken and yogurt.
2 Put the chicken pieces in the bowl and sprinkle with the salt. Pour over the yogurt and turn the chicken pieces to coat thoroughly. Cover and leave to marinate for 2 hours.
3 Crush the saffron threads in your fingers. Drop them into a cup measure and half-fill with boiling water. Let soak for at least 2 hours to release color and flavor, then strain the liquid.
4 Put the poppy seeds, cinnamon, chili powder, coriander seeds, cumin and pepper with the water

into a coffee grinder (see Cook's tip) or the goblet of a blender and work for 1-2 minutes until thoroughly combined into a spicy paste.
5 Melt the ghee in a large saucepan. Add the onion and sauté gently for about 3 minutes. ☐ Add the garlic and ginger and cook for a further 2 minutes. Stir in the spicy paste, add the cardamom pods and cloves and cook for a further 1 minute.
6 Add the chicken pieces with the yogurt and the strained saffron liquid. Heat to just below the boiling point and cover tightly. Lower heat and simmer very gently for 1½ hours.
7 Stir in the cashew nuts and cream and simmer for a further 15 minutes. Transfer to a warmed serving dish, garnish with coriander and serve.

TO SKIN CHICKEN

Use a clean dish towel to hold the skin as you pull it away from the flesh, to give a firmer grip.

Cook's Notes

TIME
Allow 2 hours marinating and soaking the saffron. Preparation, including precooking, takes 15 minutes. Cooking the *korma* takes a total of 1¾ hours.

WATCHPOINT
Do not overcook the onions at this stage. They should be soft but not brown. All the color in the dish should come from the bright golden saffron.

SERVING IDEAS
Boiled rice is good with Chicken *korma*, but for a change serve *naan* – the flat leavened bread that is traditionally baked in India in the tandoor clay oven. *Naan* bread is available from Indian and Greek specialist food stores. Alternatively, serve poppadoms, which are now available plain or garlic or curry flavored.

COOK'S TIPS
If you do a lot of Indian cooking, it is well worth keeping a coffee grinder specially for grinding the spices which are the essential feature of this cuisine, or invest in a mortar and pestle to work the spices. Both methods will release the essential oils of the spices.

BUYING GUIDE
If you cannot find fresh ginger, available from some supermarkets and oriental stores, use ½ teaspoon ground ginger instead.

DID YOU KNOW
Chicken *korma* was originally made with yogurt only, giving a dish with less sauce – *korma* means "dry". As cream became more widely used in India, it was added to increase the richness of the dish.

● 605 calories per portion

Rogan Josh is a spiced lamb dish which is popular throughout the Muslim areas of Northern India and the North West Frontier – each region having its own version. *Sag Aloo*, a delicious spicy blend of spinach and chunky potatoes, is a popular vegetable accompaniment.

Rogan Josh

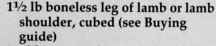

SERVES 4

1½ lb boneless leg of lamb or lamb shoulder, cubed (see Buying guide)
3 tablespoons ghee or vegetable oil (see Buying guide)
8 whole black peppercorns
3 cloves
4 cardamom seeds
1 whole dried chili pepper (optional)
1 tablespoon shredded coconut
3 tablespoons finely ground almonds
2 tablespoons ground coriander
1 tablespoon ground cumin
1 teaspoon ground turmeric
¼ teaspoon freshly grated nutmeg
¼ teaspoon ground mace
½ cup water
1 inch piece fresh gingerroot, peeled and finely chopped
2 cloves garlic, minced
1 onion, minced
1 teaspoon salt
3 tablespoons plain yogurt
1 can (8 oz) tomatoes

1 Heat 2 tablespoons of ghee in a large saucepan, add peppercorns, cloves, cardamom seeds and the chili pepper, if using, and sauté over moderate heat for 1-2 minutes until they start to darken.

2 Add the meat and sauté for 5 minutes to brown on all sides. Remove from the heat, drain off and reserve any liquid. Set aside the liquid and the meat.
3 Preheat the broiler to high. In a bowl mix together the coconut, almonds, coriander and cumin. Spread out in the broiler pan and broil until the mixture starts to brown. ⚠ Stir once or twice to brown evenly. Transfer the mixture to a bowl and mix in the turmeric, nutmeg, mace, the reserved liquid from the meat and the water and set aside.
4 Heat the remaining ghee in a skillet, add ginger and garlic and cook gently for 1-2 minutes. Add the onion and cook for about 5 minutes until soft and lightly colored.
5 Stir in the coconut and spice paste and cook for 2 minutes, stirring constantly. Add the salt, yogurt and the tomatoes and their juice. Bring to a boil, lower the heat and simmer for 5 minutes.
6 Pour the mixture over the meat and spices in the saucepan and stir well. Bring to a boil, then lower the heat and simmer gently for about 1¼-1½ hours, stirring the meat and sauce occasionally.
7 Remove the dried chili pepper, if used, and transfer Rogan Josh to warmed serving dish. Serve at once with Sag Aloo (see recipe).

Sag Aloo

SERVES 4

1 can (16 oz) spinach, drained
½ lb potatoes, cut in chunks
2 tablespoons ghee or vegetable oil
6 whole black peppercorns
2 cardamom seeds
1 fresh red chili, seeded and finely shredded
1 inch fresh gingerroot, peeled and cut in small matchsticks
½ onion, sliced
1 clove garlic, crushed
1 teaspoon ground coriander
1 teaspoon ground cumin
salt
3 tablespoons water

1 Heat the ghee in a saucepan, add the peppercorns and cardamom seeds and sauté for 2-3 minutes.
2 Add the chili, ginger, onion and garlic to the pan and cook for a further 3-4 minutes.
3 Stir in the spices and salt and mix well. Add the potatoes and the water. Bring to a boil, then lower the heat and simmer for 5 minutes, stirring occasionally.
4 Gently stir in the spinach, then simmer for about 30 minutes until the potatoes are tender.

Cook's Notes

Rogan Josh

TIME
Preparation takes about 30 minutes and cooking 1¼-1½ hours. The dish can be prepared in advance to the end of stage 5. Let stand after adding the cooked paste, yogurt and tomatoes to meat.

COOK'S TIP
The flavor of spices varies according to the way they are prepared; quickly sautéing the whole spices and toasting the ground spices gives the authentic Indian taste to this delicious lamb dish.

WATCHPOINT
Take great care when toasting the nuts and spices under the broiler as they brown very quickly. As soon as they begin to color, stir with a wooden spoon to brown the nuts and spices underneath.

●565 calories per portion

BUYING GUIDE
You will need about 2-2½ lb meat on the bone to get 1½ lb lean meat. A small leg is the best cut for this recipe as it has far less fat than a shoulder.

Ghee is an Indian cooking fat which can be made either from clarified butter or vegetable fat. It is easily obtainable from specialist Indian food stores.

DID YOU KNOW
Outside India spiced dishes like these are known as curries, derived from the Tamil word *kari*, meaning "a sauce". In India each dish is known by its own name.

SERVING IDEAS
Serve with Sag Aloo, boiled rice, a selection of chutneys and relishes and raita: Mix 1¼ cups plain yogurt with pared shredded cucumber, seasoned with salt and black pepper. Serve with mango chutney, hot lime pickle, tomato relish, grated carrot and banana salad, and chopped onions mixed with chili powder.

Sag Aloo

TIME
Preparing and cooking take about 45 minutes. The Sag Aloo can be prepared and cooked after the Rogan Josh has started to cook.

VARIATION
Frozen spinach can be used in place of canned. Substitute two packages (10 oz size) frozen chopped spinach. Let thaw, retaining all the liquid. Add a little more water if the Sag Aloo shows signs of drying out during cooking.

SERVING IDEAS
This spicy vegetable dish can be served with any curried meat dish.

●135 calories per portion

AUSTRALIA

Carpetbag steak, thick-cut beef steak stuffed with oysters, was very popular in Victorian England. It travelled successfully with the early settlers to Australia, where the abundance of prime beef and large juicy oysters established it as a firm favorite. Today it is still a much-appreciated dinner-party dish in Australia, and is excellent stuffed with mussels – as here – which are much less expensive than oysters.

Carpetbag steak

SERVES 4

1½ lb rump or sirloin steak, in one piece, about 2 inches thick, trimmed of excess fat (see Buying guide)
24 fresh mussels (see Buying guide)
6 tablespoons water
6 tablespoons dry white wine
salt and freshly ground black pepper
2 sprigs fresh thyme or ½ teaspoon dried thyme
2 leaves fresh sage or ½ teaspoon dried sage
2 tablespoons vegetable oil
1 tablespoon lemon juice
1 tablespoon chopped fresh parsley
1 tablespoon dry sherry

1 Prepare the mussels: Remove the beards, scrub the shells well and discard any that are opened.
2 Cook the mussels: Place them in a large saucepan with the water and wine. Bring to a boil, cover and cook over high heat for 4-5 minutes, shaking the pan often, until all the shells are opened (see Watchpoint page 55). Drain and leave until cool enough to handle, then prise the mussels out of the shells with a small, very sharp knife. Pat dry with absorbent kitchen paper.
3 Season the steak with salt and pepper. Fill the pocket with the drained cooked mussels and secure the edges of the steak with wooden cocktail picks.
4 Place the thyme and sage in a shallow earthenware dish and carefully lay the mussel-stuffed steak on top. Mix the oil with the lemon juice and pour over the steak. Leave to marinate for at least 1 hour, turning

the steak in the herb marinade after 30 minutes.
5 Preheat the oven to 225°F. Preheat the broiler to moderate.
6 Lift the steak from the marinade and lay it on the broiler rack. Broil the steak, basting often with the marinade mixture and turning it carefully with kitchen tongs midway through cooking time, until done to your liking; 8 minutes on each side for rare meat; 10-12 minutes for medium meat; 15 minutes for well done meat.
7 When the steak is cooked, transfer to a warmed serving dish then remove and discard the cocktail picks. Keep the broiled steak hot in the oven.
8 Turn the broiler to high. Add the parsley and sherry to the juices in the broiler pan and heat quickly under the broiler. Pour the juices over the cooked steak.
9 Serve the steak hot, cut in slices so that there is a portion of mussel filling in each slice.

PREPARING STEAK FOR STUFFING

Make a pocket in the steak by slitting horizontally: Cut through one long edge and to within ½ inch of the other three edges.

Cook's Notes

TIME
Allow 2-3 hours thawing time if using frozen mussels. Cooking the mussels takes about 5 minutes, stuffing the steak about 5 minutes. Allow 1 hour marinating time. Cooking then takes about 15-30 minutes and finishing the dish about 3 minutes.

BUYING GUIDE
Ask your butcher for well-hung Porterhouse steak or flat bone sirloin, about 2 inches thick. Ask him to cut a deep pocket for the mussel stuffing by slitting the steak lengthwise, starting at one long edge and cutting through to within not more than ½ inch of the other 3 edges. This is a fairly delicate operation, requiring considerable skill and a razor-sharp knife, and if you are unsure then ask the butcher to prepare the pocket for you.
If fresh mussels are not available, use 1 can (8 oz), well drained. Cultivated mussels, now on sale in good supermarkets, need only a good rinsing before cooking.

SERVING IDEAS
In the Australian tradition, serve this steak at a barbecue with a green salad and buttered jacket potatoes – start cooking the potatoes before you cook the steak. Australian wines are becoming increasingly available and make a good accompaniment to this dish.

●305 calories per portion

Pavlova was created and named by a society hostess in honor of the famous ballerina Anna Pavlova during a tour of Australia. One of Australia's favorite national dishes, it is a wonderfully light and rich combination of meringue, whipped cream and fruit. Perfect for a special dinner party, it is, however, so popular with the Australians that they would be just as likely to serve it for an informal barbecue in the garden for family or friends.

In Australia, Pavlova is often filled with juicy, orange-yellow passion fruit, which is readily available, but it is just as successful filled with other fruits such as strawberries, ripe peaches and kiwi fruit which have soft textures and bright colors to contrast with the meringue.

A less well-known version, but one that is equally popular in Australia, is Lemon Pavlova, in which the meringue case is exactly the same as the traditional Pavlova, but the fruit and cream are replaced by a tangy lemon filling which makes a lovely piquant contrast to the sweetness of the meringue. It also provides an excellent way of using up the egg yolks (left over from the meringue) and is more suited to winter climates when soft fruits are not available. If you prefer the fruit and cream filling, however, simply make the meringue case as below and fill with 1¼ cups sweet whipped cream and the fruits of your choice.

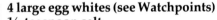

Pavlova

SERVES 6
MERINGUE SHELL
4 large egg whites (see Watchpoints)
¼ teaspoon salt
½ cup granulated sugar
½ cup superfine sugar
1 teaspoon cornstarch
½ teaspoon distilled white vinegar
lemon rind, to decorate

LEMON FILLING
4 large egg yolks
¼ cup superfine sugar
¼ cup lemon juice
1 tablespoon grated lemon rind
¾ cup whipping cream

1 Preheat the oven to 225°F.
2 With a pencil, lightly draw an 8 inch circle on a sheet of non-stick parchment or foil. Place on a baking sheet or cut out first (see Illustration).
3 Make the meringue shell: Put the egg whites into a large bowl, making sure that it is spotlessly clean and thoroughly dry.
4 With a balloon whip, beat the egg whites and salt until standing in stiff peaks (see Illustration). Gradually beat in the granulated sugar, 1 tablespoon at a time, beating until the sugar is thoroughly dissolved.
5 Sift the superfine sugar with the cornstarch and, using a metal spoon, fold mixture into the beaten egg whites. Finally, fold in the vinegar.
6 Spread a ¾ inch layer of meringue evenly over the circle drawn on the paper, on the baking sheet. Build the rest of the meringue up to form the sides of the shell, using a spoon or a pastry bag fitted with a large plain tip.
7 Bake the meringue shell in the oven for 2-2½ hours until the meringue is crisp and just very lightly colored.
8 Meanwhile, make the filling: Beat the egg yolks in a bowl until foamy. Slowly beat in the superfine sugar, then the lemon juice and rind. Transfer to the top of a double boiler or a heatproof bowl set snugly over a saucepan of simmering water. Stir until the mixture is thick and smooth; it is ready when it slides cleanly straight from the spoon, without trickling. (This is a slow process and can take as long as 10 minutes.) Let stand until quite cold.
9 When the meringue is baked, remove from the oven and let cool slightly, then very carefully peel away the paper from the base. Place the meringue shell on a flat serving platter to cool completely, ready for filling.
10 When both meringue and lemon filling are cold, whip the cream until thick and fold into lemon filling. Spoon into center of the meringue shell, top with a little lemon rind and serve at room temperature.

Cook's Notes

TIME
Preparing the meringue shell takes about 45 minutes; making the filling and baking the meringue takes 2-2½ hours. Both the meringue and the filling require a further 30 minutes to cool.

WATCHPOINTS
Use eggs at room temperature, not straight from the refrigerator. Cold egg whites do not give as great a volume when beaten. Take great care when separating the whites from the yolks; any trace of yolk will prevent the white from foaming.

FREEZING
The Lemon Pavlova freezes well. Preferably the meringue shell should be made in an 8½ inch foil plate, not on a sheet of paper. Fill the meringue shell and flash freeze before placing in a large rigid container. Alternatively, the meringue shell can be frozen unfilled, then thawed at room temperature for about 1 hour and filled when ready to serve. Lemon Pavlova, filled and unfilled, can be stored for up to 2 months in the freezer.

●320 calories per portion

MAKING MERINGUE SHELL AND LEMON FILLING

1 Beat the egg whites until they are stiff enough to stay in position if the bowl is turned upside down.

2 Spread meringue evenly over circle of paper and spoon or pipe the rest to form the sides.

3 The lemon mixture is ready when it will slide cleanly straight from the spoon without trickling.

INDEX

Picture Credits